CIRCLES WITHOUT CENTER

# CIRCLES WITHOUT CENTER

## PATHS TO THE DISCOVERY

## AND CREATION OF SELF

## IN MODERN LITERATURE

*Enrico Garzilli*

HARVARD UNIVERSITY PRESS

Cambridge, Massachusetts

1972

PN
771
.G3
1972

Fairleigh Dickinson
University Library

Teaneck, New Jersey

© Copyright 1972 by the President and Fellows of Harvard College
All rights reserved
Library of Congress Catalog Card Number 77-182814
SBN 674-13165-7
Printed in the United States of America

So far, I have found no stable or definite centre in the unconscious and I don't believe such a centre exists. I believe that the thing which I call the Self is an ideal centre, equidistant between the Ego and the Unconscious, and it is probably equivalent to the maximum natural expression of individuality, in a state of fulfilment or totality. As nature aspires to express itself, so does man, and the Self is that dream of totality.

The self . . . is a circle whose centre is everywhere and whose circumference is nowhere.

—C. G. Jung in *C. G. Jung & Hermann Hesse*

# PREFACE

This book explores the paths to the discoveries and creations of self in contemporary literature. The introduction discusses the problem of the loss of identity of modern man in terms of how even man's best images, his heroes, have suffered their eclipse. The question of the real in what is an illusively psychological subject is also explored here. The rest of the book deals with "anti-heroes" and the fragments of self through which the personages search for survival. The first chapter finds man alone journeying inward; the second chapter recognizes the need for other people in this quest. Other people inevitably bring in the problem of language and public masks; the third and fourth chapters consequently treat these aspects. Since the person's meanderings become maze-like, often symbolic not only of his quest but of his own labyrinthine existence, the fifth chapter deals with the myth of the labyrinth and the self. Eventually man finds that his identity is not simply discovered but created; this is explored through the dynamic quality of the characters in literature and in the transcendent and immanent creativity of their authors. The last chapter discusses the changes in literary form as reflecting and mirroring evolving man. The conclusion treats synthetically the different avenues of explorations found in the prologue to St. John's Gospel (treated in its mythical dimensions as literature). John's prologue serves as an introduction to the person of Christ in a way that this book humbly hopes will begin an exploration into the finite-infinite modern self. Very little explicit biographical material is found in the book; authorial life is present usually only implicitly in the search, journey, and existence of the creator's characters.

# Preface

I am profoundly grateful to Albert Salvan and Edwin Honig for their insights, suggestions, and inspiration all during the preparation of this work. I also appreciate the help and encouragement given to me by Juan López-Morillas and Mark Spilka.

I am indebted to many others—to Raymond Hanson for his editorial help, to Rev. Basil De Pinto and Raymond Hanson for their help with the translations, to Ronald Brassard and Michael Leckie for their typing, to Yvonne Murray not only for her generosity and patience in typing but for her constant reassurances about the worth of the undertaking.

The author wishes gratefully to acknowledge permission to translate and use material from the following works:

*Così è (se vi pare)* by Luigi Pirandello, copyright © 1918 by Nuova Antologia, copyright, Luigi Pirandello. By permission of the Pirandello Estate.

*Enrico IV,* copyright © 1922 by R. Bemporad e F., copyright by Luigi Pirandello. By permission of the Pirandello Estate.

*Sei personaggi in cerca d'autore,* copyright © 1921 by R. Bemporad e F., copyright by Luigi Pirandello. By permission of the Pirandello Estate.

*The Unnamable* by S. Beckett. Translated from the French by the author. Copyright © 1958 by Grove Press, Inc. Reprinted by permission of Grove Press, Inc.

*Poems in English* by S. Beckett. Copyright © 1961 by Samuel Beckett. Reprinted by permission of Grove Press, Inc.

*Waiting for Godot: Tragicomedy in 2 acts* by S. Beckett. Translated from the original French text by the author. Copyright © 1954 by Grove Press. Reprinted by permission of Grove Press, Inc. and Faber & Faber, Ltd.

*Endgame: A Play in One Act* by S. Beckett. Translated from the French by the author. Copyright © 1958 by Grove Press, Inc. Reprinted by permission of Grove Press, Inc. and Faber & Faber, Ltd.

*How It Is* by S. Beckett. Translated from the French by the author. Copyright © 1964 by Grove Press, Inc. Reprinted by permission of Grove Press, Inc.

*Murphy* by S. Beckett. First published 1938. First Grove Press Edition 1957. All rights reserved. Reprinted by permission of Grove Press, Inc.

*Happy Days: A Play in Two Acts* by S. Beckett. Copyright © 1961 by Grove Press, Inc. Reprinted by permission of Grove Press, Inc. and Faber & Faber, Ltd.

*The Collected Works of Paul Valéry,* ed. by Jackson Mathews, Bollingen Series XLV, vol. 1, *Poems,* translated by David Paul (copyright © 1971

# Preface

by Princeton University Press); vol. 8, *Leonardo, Poe, Mallarmé*, translated by Malcolm Cowley and James R. Lawler (copyright © 1972 by Princeton University Press [forthcoming]); vol. 6, *Monsieur Teste*, translated by Jackson Mathews (forthcoming from Princeton University Press, which will hold the copyright to this volume). By permission of Princeton University Press and Routledge and Kegan Paul. (The translations in *Circles Without Center* are my own.)

*Absalom, Absalom!* by W. Faulkner. Copyright © 1936 by William Faulkner, © 1951 by Random House, Inc. By permission of Random House, Inc.

*The Sound and the Fury* by W. Faulkner. Copyright © 1929, 1956 by William Faulkner, © 1946 by Random House. By permission of Random House, Inc.

*As I Lay Dying* by W. Faulkner. Copyright © 1930, 1957 by William Faulkner, © 1946 by Random House, Inc. By permission of Random House, Inc.

*Les Faux Monnayeurs* by A. Gide. Copyright © 1927 by Editions Gallimard. By permission of Alfred A. Knopf, Inc.

*Thesée* by A. Gide. Copyright © 1958 by Editions Gallimard. By permission of Alfred A. Knopf, Inc.

*Journal* by A. Gide. Copyright © 1951 by Editions Gallimard. By permission of Alfred A. Knopf, Inc.

*Finnegans Wake* by James Joyce. Copyright © 1939 by James Joyce, copyright © renewed 1967 by George Joyce and Lucia Joyce. All rights reserved. By permission of Viking Press, Inc. and The Society of Authors.

*Myth and Reality* by M. Eliade. Copyright © 1963 by Harper & Row, Publishers, Inc. By permission of Harper & Row, Publishers, Inc.

*Labyrinths* by Jorge Luis Borges. Edited and translated by Donald A. Yates and James E. Irby. Copyright © 1962, 1964 by New Directions Publishing Corporation. By permission of New Directions Publishing Corporation.

*Insight* by B. Lonergan. First published, 1957, by Longmans, Green, and Co. Ltd. By permission of Philosophical Library, Inc.

*Siddhartha* by Hermann Hesse. Permission to translate and publish excerpts from *Siddhartha* granted by New Directions Publishing Corporation, publishers of Hermann Hesse, *Siddhartha,* copyright 1951 by New Directions Publishing Corporation. Published by Peter Owen in the British Commonwealth.

*Language and Myth* by Ernst Cassirer, Dover Publications Inc., New York. Reprinted through permission of the publisher.

*C. G. Jung and Hermann Hesse: A Record of Two Friendships* by Miguel Serrano. Copyright © 1966 by Miguel Serrano. Reprinted by permission of Schocken Books, Inc. and Routledge and Kegan Paul, Ltd.

# Preface

*Le Voyeur* by A. Robbe-Grillet. Copyright © 1958 by Grove Press, Inc. By permission of Grove Press, Inc. and Les Editions de Minuit.

*Dans le labyrinthe* by A. Robbe-Grillet. Copyright © 1960, 1965, by Grove Press, Inc. By permission of Grove Press, Inc. and Les Editions de Minuit.

*Pour un nouveau roman* by A. Robbe-Grillet. Copyright © 1965. By permission of Grove Press, Inc. and Les Editions de Minuit.

Providence, 1972                                    Enrico Garzilli

# CONTENTS

# Contents

## CIRCLES WITHOUT CENTER

> These our actors,
> As I foretold you, were all spirits, and
> Are melted into air, into thin air;
> And, like the baseless fabric of this vision,
> The cloud-capp'd towers, the gorgeous palaces,
> The solemn temples, the great globe itself,
> Yea, all which it inherit, shall dissolve
> And, like this insubstantial pageant faded,
> Leave not a rack behind. We are such stuff
> As dreams are made on, and our little life
> Is rounded with a sleep.

—Shakespeare, *The Tempest*

# INTRODUCTION

What it means to be a person has become the object of much contemporary writing. Psychologists, sociologists, philosophers, and theologians all contribute their viewpoints toward a better understanding of personhood. At the same time that these writers encourage a deepening awareness of growth into personhood, they are conscious of the many difficulties which present themselves. Alienation, loss of identity, fragmentation are frequent descriptions for the tensions in the experience of contemporary man. In fact, one critic calls the anonymous hero or stranger modern man's prototype.[1] Her thesis finds confirmation in much of contemporary literature. For instance, Roquentin, the protagonist of Sartre's *La Nausée,* claims that he does not understand anything about the face he sees before him in the mirror, while Kyo of Malraux's *La Condition humaine* does not recognize his own voice on a recording. These examples not only become symbolic of anonymity or facelessness but become the prototypes for modern man's need to find himself. The search for self seems to be almost the necessary response to what has become a cliché in contemporary life, that is, the identity crisis.

In speaking about the lack of a feeling of self, the Basque philosopher Unamuno observes that one of his best friends used to remark: "But I have no sense of myself; I don't know what that is."[2] Unamuno sees the changing self as involving a continuity which results from the persistence of memory. In a discussion on what makes a man this person and not another, he calls upon the principle of unity and continuity. Unity results from the person's position in space, his action and intentionality. Continuity in time results from memory. "Memory is the basis of individual personality, just as tradition is the basis of the collective personality of a people."[3] Every change which takes place in the person, then, can only come from the security that an alteration in thinking or feeling is consistent with the self's experience of unity of spirit and of continuity. Otherwise, change, according to Unamuno, means the pathological obliteration of personality. While Unamuno may emphasize the continuity present in personality, André Gide and Marcel Proust seem to be more taken up with the changes and the many shocks of time with which the "I" has to struggle. Although, Unamuno calls consciousness a disease, other writers like Pascal and Moravia define man as the "roseau pensant" and concentrate on consciousness as his claim to dignity. All of them would agree on the tensions, ambiguities, and tragedies which consciousness encompasses. They agree, too, that man is an end and can never be treated as a means. Consciousness and the mental self become the starting point for the journey of man to himself, since, as Ernst Cassirer points out in his definition of man, consciousness makes man capable of symbolic forms.

Humanist writers persistently encourage man to become more aware of the possibilities of his growth as a person and arrive at a better understanding of the fact that he is an end rather than a means. The goal of the Greeks, "Know thyself," has, then, become more difficult for modern man to achieve; recognizing his fragmentation and his many selves, he still has the invincible need to speak out as an "I" from among all of these fragments of identity.

Linked to an understanding of man is the concept of the hero, to the extent that the hero represents the perfect or great man. Man often unconsciously looks to the hero for his own definition or measures himself against this perfect or great man. Yet both the hero and man have suffered an eclipse in contemporary experience. While man has often been reduced to a means, an object, or a thing, and is sometimes caught in the maze of his many selves, the hero has been treated as an antifactor. If there is an awareness of the evil which results from treating man as an "it" instead of a "thou" (Buber, Marcel), there is also a vacuum felt at times by the demise of the hero. New, but short-lived heroes are continually emerging from new ephemeral mythologies.[4] Yet the kind of hero that is revered is often an excellent barometer in defining the type of mythology and value system of a particular culture. While the myth and the hero may crumble together, man persists, forced, however, to see his best reflections in new myths and heroes.

There are, moreover, vast differences between the Promethean hero,

2

the Christian hero, the athlete, the cinematic hero, the space hero, the guru, or more perverse still, the white Western hero. In a critical approach to himself, man is forced to re-evaluate and reassess all these "best definitions" of himself. In addition, since Greek mythology no longer exists as a collection of lived beliefs and since Christian mythology is fragmented, contemporary man sees himself at his best only in vestiges of these former myths and at his worst in the more recent parodies or cults of these myths.

Whether the hero found himself in the past a rebel against order like Prometheus or the perfect expression of this order, there has always been some pattern or structure against which he could be measured. Modern man now finds himself in a world in which the former "sacred" structures are so fragmented that Greek and Christian heroes have almost vanished along with the Hegelian hero, who sacrifices personal happiness to rescue the world from chaos, and the Nietzschean superman who is obsessed with power. Those heroes who remain and those who have been recently created are being more and more critically scrutinized. For instance, Merleau-Ponty's statement "I distrust heroes" finds support in a world where man's literature seems to suggest that he sees his best reflection in the fragments of the antihero.[5]

There still are forms, however, in which "real" heroes, not antiheroes, are presented to man to be imitated. Besides the Western and the war epic, one of the literary forms is the sermon. Since the literary sermon very explicitly encourages the reader or hearer to heroism, it may be helpful to give a short analysis of this one type of hero who is still exalted and whose identity is clearly defined, in contrast to the many antiheroes such as Roquentin, Murphy, and the Unnamable found in this book. The three sermons to be considered are Fr. Mapple's in Melville's *Moby Dick,* Père Paneloux's in Camus's *La Peste,* and the hell sermon in Joyce's *A Portrait of the Artist as a Young Man.*

All three sermons have in common the difficulties and sufferings involved in obeying the inscrutable will of God, the evil that befalls men in disobeying it, and the necessity for hatred of self as a remedy against pride. The truly heroic man, then, must submit himself to the divine order. Fr. Mapple tells his congregation that they must learn how to be humble to God's will: "But all the things that God would have us do are hard for us to do . . . And if we obey God, we must disobey ourselves."[6] The disobedience of ourselves which is the elimination of pride, he suggests, constitutes the difficult path to sainthood or heroism. Paneloux in *La Peste* echoes almost verbatim the advice of Mapple: "Love of

3

God is a difficult love. It means the total abandonment of oneself to God and self-hate.''[7]

Arnall insists in *Portrait* that the greatest evil man can do is to sin through pride.[8] The opposite of ''disobeying ourselves'' (Mapple), and ''dédain de sa personne'' (Paneloux), pride repeats the independence and self-love which caused Lucifer and Adam and Eve to speak out their ''Non serviam'': ''I will not serve.''

While all three sermons vary on the degree of inscrutability in God's will, they emphasize the necessity for self-disobedience in heroism. Mapple uses the example of Jonah's punishment in the whale for his willful disobedience to God. The preacher in *Portrait* cites Lucifer and Adam and Eve and continues by illustrating real heroism in the perfect obedience to God's will exemplified in Jesus of Nazareth. In other words, the perfect man realizes that in spite of its inscrutability real heroism results from fidelity to God's will and to preordained structure.

This preordained structure seems, however, to be involved with the torturous problem of innocent suffering. Camus's Paneloux stresses a theme consistent in literature since Job: that is, the problem of evil in innocent suffering. In spite of the suffering and the death of children, Paneloux claims real sanctity, heroism, is possible through faith. God alone knows why He permits this suffering. Man can only submit through belief since his road to salvation and heroism is a road of mystery and obedience to the mysteries of an order which transcend man's understanding. Yet, another important aspect of heroism is that which seems to stress the very opposite of fidelity to order and that is the individual mission. In reading Job, Melville had underlined another reason for heroism; for while Job said he would trust God even if slain by Him, he would ''*maintain his own ways before Him.*'' This allusion certainly reflects the importance of the individual mission for a man to be considered truly heroic. Fidelity to his individuality is what constitutes the fabric of heroism. Prometheus, for instance, was an enemy of Zeus only after he had stolen the fire. He worked with Zeus as a friend in defeating the old order and the old god, Ouranos. The significant point, however, is that the rebellion of Prometheus begins early in his heroic career and points to the importance of individuality in the mission of the hero. The consequence of individuality, then, so long as it does not permanently say ''Non serviam,'' means, ironically, service in a different way. Even instances in the life of Christ, who is the truly heroic example of the sermon, seem to demonstrate a revolutionary stance toward order because of a unique mission from His Father. This mission transcends the ordinary order over which the hero towers. These different aspects of the hero always present a certain embarrassment to the sermonist who emphasizes only submission. Yet, the real hero and saint have always felt themselves larger than the structures around them and in some instances have demonstrated real rebellion in following their own path.

The problems which the heroic evoke are central to the experience of man. Innocent suffering, the personal mission versus the inscrutable preordained order will always find sympathetic resonances in man. Their force resides in the fact that they symbolically represent values which transcend the particular mythologies and deal with the problems which man always has to confront. To the extent that he experiences these values and problems he can still discover orientation in the vestiges of heroic example found in Job, Prometheus, and Christ.

Yet, for contemporary man these heroes are not completely credible. He is living in a universe which seems to him at times to have lost a structure and a transcendent meaning. And rebellion, since it is always grounded in a unique mission, has some type of structure against which to measure itself. Heroism also requires the passage of time to evaluate. While there may be some figures living today whom history may genuinely view as the great men, such as campus radicals and black revolutionaries, the perspective which will allow them to be more universally accepted has yet to be provided by time. Moreover, since a transcendent order and a preordained will seem to be obscure elements in modern life, man to determine his personal path sometimes seeks a surrogate in astrology.

If contemporary man finds himself often described in literature as the fragmented antihero, as a man with many selves, these descriptions must indeed be suggestive of his own life. While man has always recognized fragmentation within himself, not since the rise of psychological theology has he so consciously adverted to the fact that his demons and gods are sometimes the personification of the forces within him. The breakdown of a structured universe based on either Christian or Greek mythology, the rise of psychology, the absurd tragedies of world wars, and the always present possibility of cataclysm make man even more aware of the fragments of selves he sees within him and finds himself creating.

In looking into himself man wonders where his real self is. He may seek to reassure himself that his real self is his consciousness, implicit in so many definitions of man. He may also wonder what function his roles in society and other people have to play concerning self, in terms of a personality that seems so inconstant. Sometimes, he may even seem to himself lost in a maze of possibilities, struggling to discern reality from unreality, dream from consciousness.

What does the real "me" or "I" mean in this context? This question, so much a part of the problem of what is the real, forces man to confront that most basic of all questions. As man is asking himself what is the real "I," he is implicitly asking what is the real; a short analysis of the various meanings of the real may shed some light on the question. For another way of asking why are great men of the past no longer heroic to modern man may be to ask why are they no longer a reality for so much of contemporary experience.

A knowledge of the progression of the real from the debates on the universal to the psychological real shows an evolution which can be helpful in understanding the presumed psychologically real which this book explores. The connection between realism and the concrete individual person was recognized in the great debates in the medieval schools of the twelfth century. The battle between William of Champeaux, the realist, and Peter Abelard, the quasi nominalist, centers around the separate existence of universals versus reality as founded only in particular or proper names. Abelard's *Historia Calamitatum* is an expression of a methodology which begins with the particular and marks a rediscovery of the uniqueness of personality. Since Augustine's *Confessions* the concept of a personality viewed as unique to each individual had been blurred in the undifferentiated category of man. *Historia Calamitatum,* Abelard's autobiography, reveals a particular man whose story, because of its uniqueness, can never be confused with that of another man. Abelard's position, however, was not termed realism since it was opposed to the realism of William of Champeaux who defined the universal category as the only real.

As the Platonic belief in the separate existence of universals waned and nominalism became more diffused, the definition of the real shifted to the concrete thing. The real became identified with the particular man, Peter, for instance, rather than simply the universal man. Watt sees the relation between the name and identity as significant: "Logically the problem of individual identity is closely related to the epistemological status of proper names . . . [Proper names] are the verbal expressions of the particular identity of each person."[9] Watt suggests that modern realism finds its roots in Descartes and Locke. He states that the form of the novel is the literary genre which most fully reflects and results from the individualistic point of view. Since in this case perception becomes the immediate test of truth, the epistemological context of point of view relates selection to ontology. For instance, the subjects become more real in the Goncourts (Edward Goncourt, 1871) if they come from the lower depths of society. The real in Zola's methodology comes from an imitation of the scientific, which places emphasis on observation and experimentation and reveals heredity and environment as the determinants of personality. From objects which are available to scientific testing to the symbols of the imagination, the definition of the real evolves. The symbolists, for instance, suggest that the immediate symbols of the imagination reflect a deeper reality. Impressionism in painting and music, the psychological data of Freud and Jung continue to show that the conscious point of view is not the only real but that the subconscious and the dream are also real. Einstein's doctrine confirms the epistemological expression of the relativity of point of view in space and time. The real then also becomes the expression of a relative point of view. Ortega y Gasset, Lawrence Durrell, Dostoevsky, James Joyce, and Marcel Proust, for example, express in verbal art the truths of psychological realism; that is, that dreams, independent time series, and the illogicality of one's thought life are reality.

An understanding of psychological realism in the whole context of the development of the real from the universal real to the present is presupposed in this study. Also helpful as an example in the psychological reality of the many selves is the double in Dostoevsky. Dimitri Chizhevsky, for instance, sees the splitting of Ivan's personality in *The Brothers Karamazov* as a result of the nonacceptance of the particular and the concrete.[10]

The fragmentation of the individual is a persistent theme, then, in literature and psychology. Contemporary man has gone beyond limiting the experience of the real to the problem of the individual, since he now sees within him many selves, some, he believes, more real than others. From another point of view he now asks which self is the real "I."

This study not only presupposes an understanding of realism but also presents a psychological subject in a literary context. There can always be further questions concerning selection of works. The study humbly expects to be a beginning of an exploration of the many selves of modern man.

This book seeks the path to the real self. Sometimes it may be a very explicit quest as in Hermann Hesse's *Siddhartha* when the pilgrim asks the question about the real self in this way: "But where, where was this innermost, ultimate I? It was not flesh and bone, it was not thought or consciousness, the wise men taught. Where then, where was it?''[11] At other times it may be a subtle labyrinthine quest to recover human presence in a world dominated by objects as in *Dans le labyrinthe* by Robbe-Grillet. This study becomes a kind of pilgrimage in search of the self and the creation of the self. It reveals man searching for himself alone, within himself, in his relationships to other people, in his language and myths, in his dreams, in his creativity, and in his creations. These are all different routes to the many selves in which man must seek his identity. As the study progresses, not only does the pilgrim find that his path becomes labyrinthine because of the maze outside, but also because the maze is within him. Many times the path seems to become circular as it unfolds before him. The journey and the pilgrim, the dream and the dreamer become one as man explores a circle whose circumference seems to be everywhere and whose center seems to be nowhere. This circle is himself; it finds its many surfaces in consciousness, in other people, in his language, his personae, and his dreams. Enclosed in two interlocking circles, a symbol for the labyrinth as well as for infinity, man learns that his real self is not simply discovered but created. He remains forever in the act of creating himself, in dialogue with others, moving on from stage to stage of self. In a letter to Jung, M. Serrano expresses the enigma of self metaphorically as a circle that carries man to the threshold of his existence where he is both creator and created, dreamer and dream:

Perhaps then in the act of listening we can arrive at that mysterious centre, which as you have said, appears to have no existence at all and seems to be something invented by ourselves; but which, nevertheless dominates us—to the extent that without it we are nothing. Without it, we are the dead burying the dead. In a way, that mysterious centre is our son, but at the same time it is our father. The Son who is the Father, the Self.[12]

8

# 1 / MAN ALONE

This study does not intend to be a technical psychological work, but it certainly presents psychological information since it examines the experience of man in literature. At times the various selves which are explored in the search for self seem to be a study of the many selves of the schizophrenic or the psychotic. In fact, as the schizoid condition of the psychologically ill in our society is better understood, psychologists also seem to understand better the various selves that even the healthy must recognize. In spite of the many selves and roles which are part of this experience, the healthy individual, Erikson insists, can still speak out an I.[1] This situation is quite different from the schizophrenic in Laing's *The Divided Self* who claims "she's an I looking for a me."[2] Although both the healthy individual and the psychotic recognize the many selves and roles, the former testifies to a more reasonably coherent self. This study seeks to transcend the categories generally associated with sanity and insanity and consider the experience of man, for the fragmentation and isolation which are part of so much of contemporary experience force most persons to confront the problem of finding and creating a reasonably coherent self.

For Erikson this secure sense of identity is best described when it can speak out of complicated experiences and say as William James does in a letter to his wife: "This is the real me!"[3] The problem of the "real me" finds its crisis in adolescence but is also an adult problem. Indeed, it is often more consciously experienced by adults, either because they have never really overcome their adolescent crisis or because of the disorienting experience of contemporary life.[4]

This chapter explores man's journey to self as he isolates himself from others. The reader of literature finds Narcissus almost the proto-type of the man alone, self-inclosed in his own image. While Narcissus to psychologists has chiefly a pejorative meaning, the meaning under-lying the imagery of the myth has not always been understood this way. Louise Vinge in her study of the Ovidian tradition claims that with the Schlegel brothers a new attitude toward the individual and toward self-knowledge gives the Narcissus myth a new understanding. ''It becomes a symbol of the ability of the creative genius to come to know the deep-est spiritual forces within himself.''[5] Even earlier than that, the theo-logical interpretation of the Second Person of the Blessed Trinity who is the *Imago Ipsius Bonitatis* of the Father echoes the Narcissus myth in its positive meaning. Interpretations of the myth of course vary from age to age. They oscillate between the negative, even homosexual, inter-pretations of the myth, and the much more positive emphasis on Narcis-sus as a creative symbol. The relationship between Narcissus and the self is central to both kinds of interpretation of the myth. Narcissus exclaims after he views his own image ''How gladly would I from my-self remove!''[6] Wishing absent that which he desires most, Narcissus is in love with just one of his selves, his bodily self, and is not able to keep it and himself from the same fate. Identified with one fragment of him-self Narcissus falls victim to Tiresias's prophecy; that is, if he ever knows himself, he surely will die. The knowledge that Narcissus has of himself is incomplete. He is alone and consequently does not have the comprehension of himself which others could bring to him. In a contemporary echo of the myth Roquentin, the protagonist of Sartre's *Nausea,* exclaims that he does not even recognize his own face because he is alone and needs other people in the structuring of his identity: ''Perhaps it is impossible to understand one's own face. Or perhaps it is because I am a single man? People who live in society have learned how to see themselves in mirrors as they appear to their friends. I have no friends.''[7] Yet since Narcissus does recognize some aspect of himself, he represents perhaps the beginning of the search for identity.

While there may be many resonances of the Narcissus myth in con-temporary literature this study concentrates particularly on two char-acters who in some way echo Narcissus in being alone in their search for self: Paul Valéry's Monsieur Teste and Samuel Beckett's Murphy. This aloneness sometimes means not only the exclusion of other people, the absence of personal relationships, the shunning of society, but more pre-cisely the search in consciousness for the real ''me.''

## Man Alone

## MONSIEUR TESTE—PAUL VALÉRY

Monsieur Teste of Paul Valéry is an example of a man who seeks himself in the aloneness of his consciousness. While the work in which Monsieur Teste is the central character does not necessarily constitute Paul Valéry's greatest contribution to letters, the problems generated by the modus vivendi of the character of Monsieur Teste reflect a lifelong preoccupation of Valéry.[8] The tension between the interior person and the person who recognizes outside reality is a significant theme in his writing and poetry from his early work on Leonardo da Vinci to *La Jeune Parque* and *Mon Faust*. *Mon Faust,* perhaps, most perfectly integrates the polarity of this tension: the tension between the internal and the external, between the body and the mind. As early as *Introduction à la méthode de Léonard de Vinci,* Paul Valéry seeks to expose the dynamics of consciousness present in the man of genius, the universal man. He finds that the problem of genius in a particular man leads inevitably to a statement on what it means to be a person. If a man of genius, for instance, were compared to one of inferior intelligence, the structural relationship in their consciousness would show that only accidental differences exist between them. He chooses, however, to study the man of genius, because in him the act of consciousness and the act of being most perfectly coincide: "There is no act of genius which is not *inferior* to the act of being. The imbecile is grounded in a magnificent principle which also dwells within him; the most talented mind contains nothing superior to this."[9]

Although Valéry uses the universal man as a starting point to show the structure of consciousness, he understands that consciousness is what identifies man with his fellow man. The law of phenomenological distinction between individuals almost seems annihilated when the structure of consciousness is explored. To illustrate this, Valéry uses the myth of the person of Leonardo da Vinci as his starting point in demonstrating that consciousness is what makes man a person and forms his participation in the act of being: "In fact, I have given the names *man* and *Leonardo* to what I conceived of as the power of the mind."[10]

The question of what it means to be a person is inextricably bound up with the nature of consciousness.

> The character of man is consciousness; and the character of conciousness is a perpetual reaching out and moving beyond, a never-ending and uncompromising detachment from everything that

comes within its grasp. It is an inexhaustible act, independent of both the quality and quantity of the things which appear in its light; and through it the man of the spirit must in the end knowingly reduce himself to an unqualified refusal to be anything whatsoever.[11]

This passage suggests several relationships that must be clarified in the refinement of what Valéry means by person : the relationship of the individual mind to the whole of consciousness, the relationship of matter to mind, or of objectivity to subjectivity, the relationship of one man's consciousness to that of another. The question of personal identity, consequently, must take into consideration the interrelationships of consciousness and its objects. These objects may embrace the body sensations which relate to the individual mind, the others whom he confronts, and the things that he constantly has to face. Here the role of objects and of other persons make up the content of consciousness, the self, of the individual person and define him as distinct. Although the distinctions between the man of genius and the man of inferior intelligence may seem great, Valéry suggests that an exploration of their conscious structure reveals only accidental differences between them. The memories, experiences, habits, and culture of particular individuals, while seeming so diverse, are really to be regarded almost as accidental in defining the person in terms of consciousness. It is consciousness which man and man have in common. His personality is composed of traits which to pure consciousness are accidental. The marginal note states clearly what Valéry means by personality, and how it differs from the self :

> The personality is made up of memories, habits, tendencies, reactions. It is, in a word, a complex of the most prompt responses of a being, even though this promptitude involves a tendency to differentiation.
>
> Now all this may be regarded as accidental when compared to consciousness, whose unique property is *to be*. Quite the opposite of personality, consciousness is perfectly impersonal.[12]

The qualities which form the structure of consciousness show how men are related and identified. The accidental qualities to which each consciousness is exposed form his personality and distinguish him from others.

Since it is through consciousness that man meets his most elemental self, the study of the conscious self must exclude the distraction of other people and things. Precisely because it is consciousness which all men have in common, and which identifies one with another, the study of it should reveal what it means to be a person and have a self. Valéry pursues these questions in the person of Monsieur Teste, a character distinct from Leonardo but related to him in a most fundamental way.

Monsieur Teste is an intriguing individual who has closed himself off from the exterior world. He seeks himself in his reflections on his conscious activity. The world outside is only important insofar as it sheds light on his own identity. To read *Monsieur Teste* as a temporary rejection on Valéry's part of art, poetry, and letters is perhaps too great a simplification. While the temporary disillusionment may be true, the work itself shows an obsession with the interior man's seeking an answer to identity. The name "Teste" indicates his nature: he is "tête," the head, the pure embodiment of consciousness, who seeks to define the self in terms of consciousness; he is also "teste" meaning witness. He is a witness to things insofar as he is conscious of them, and things bear witness to his identity insofar as they act as reflectors of his consciousness: "M. Teste est le témoin . . . Conscious—Teste, Testis.''[13]

Monsieur Teste is totally turned in upon himself not for the purpose of studying himself but for reflecting upon the consciousness by which he is aware of himself. He is interested not in particularities but in the broadest possible generality. He is not interested in the contents of consciousness but in the form of consciousness itself, the structure of consciousness, the pure act of consciousness and being. Since consciousness is at the opposite pole of personality, there is no past in moments of intense consciousness: "For a man like this, the most vivid and precise of memories appears as a reality of the *present* to his mind, and the very sensation of *pastness* in such an image is accompanied by the notion that the *past* is a fact of the *present*—a kind of . . . *color* in a picture—or else the promptness of a precise and exact answer.''[14]

In his preface to *Monsieur Teste,* Paul Valéry states that Monsieur Teste is impossible. The reason for this is that Monsieur Teste is trying to capture the essence of consciousness, to perform an infinite, self-inclosed, unrestricted act of understanding. In such an act of understanding, all possible contents would be known and actualized in a presence that can only be described as eternal. This is the reason that Monsieur Teste is impossible according to Valéry in his preface:

13

Why is M. Teste impossible?—This question touches the very core of Teste's being. In fact, *it changes you into M. Teste.* For he is none other than the very demon of possibility. Concern over the totality of what he can do dominates him. He observes himself; he maneuvers, he does not want anyone else to maneuver him. He knows only two categories, which are those of consciousness reduced to its activities: *the possible and the impossible.* In this curious brain where philosophy has little to commend itself and where language is always held suspect, almost every thought is qualified by the feeling that it is provisional; scarcely anything remains but the expectation and execution of clearly defined operations.[15]

The unrestricted act of understanding means the discovery of the relationship between the known and the unknown; in such a moment Monsieur Teste would be identical with the actual principle of consciousness, pure presence, eternal.

At these moments of intense consciousness, consciousness ceases to appear as emanating from the self; rather the self, the person, seems to be a point within a transcending field of consciousness, a field which is accessible to reflective consciousness and from which vantage point the self becomes an object of consciousness, a thing. In this moment the self becomes a you and is distinguished from the I:

And yet—just how does one go about electing a personage to be called "self"—how is this inner center established? Why is it that in the theatre of the mind you are: You?—*You* and not *me?*

And so this mechanism is not the most general that could be. If it were . . . there would no longer be an *absolute I.*—But is this not precisely what M. Teste is looking for: to withdraw from the ordinary self by constantly trying to diminish, fight against, compensate for the inequality, the anisotropy of consciousness?[16]

Monsieur Teste's obsession is the isolation in consciousness of that which is permanent and depends upon nothing. In studying the dynamism of his consciousness, Monsieur Teste denies himself; he is no longer a person, he refuses to establish a center with a name. He identifies himself with "the pure self": "the pure self, the unique and monotone presence in the world of being itself; a presence which is continually recovered only to be lost again, and which sounds at the threshold of our awareness the base of the chord of our existence."[17] This pure self is identical with absolute consciousness and constitutes the ground of personality while paradoxically remaining purely impersonal; this is clearly indicated by the distinction between personality and consciousness that Valéry makes in the marginal note cited above. Personality is distinct from the consciousness which is its ground. Consciousness is what men have in common. It is essential to man's being a man. Personality refers to what separates man, makes him unique; it is comprised of accidental qualities: "And this thing called *personality*, which we so crudely consider to be our most intimate and profound *property* and sovereign good, is merely that, a *thing*, both changeable and accidental, in stark contrast to the naked *self*; since we can think of it, calculate its interests, and even somewhat lose them from sight, personality turns out to be no more than a second-rate psychological divinity which dwells in our mirror and answers to our name."[18]

The pure ego of which Valéry speaks, then, is universal. If the individual person is able to isolate his own consciousness and trace it back, he finds that that which he names a self is simply an object in the whole of consciousness. Consequently, the one who has liberated himself from his individuality, his personality, feels himself to be pure consciousness: "In a flash the spirit which dwells in man immolates all individuality. It realizes itself as pure consciousness; there cannot be two of them. It is the *I*, the universal pronoun, the proper name of *this* which is perfectly anonymous (faceless)."[19] If an individual can transcend his personality and become identical with absolute consciousness the simultaneous existence of other individual consciousnesses becomes a problem of the one and the many.

Valéry understands that this problem of the one and the many becomes circular. It is evident that consciousness points beyond the individual person and in some way the individual can assume identity with pure consciousness and unity with the whole. At this point the reality of the ego liberated from the blurring of personality can be described in cosmic terms:

> It is not his precious *person* which he raises to this eminent height, since thought had exorcised such notions long ago; he understands that the *subject* of his acts is not *person* but *I*, the I which cannot be qualified, which has no name or history, which is no more perceptible but no less real than the center of the mass of a ring or a planetary system,—but which results from everything, whatever that everything may be.[20]

The real meaning of the whole remains shrouded in mystery, yet in some way consciousness appears to be the vital link to this understanding of the whole. For each person, since he is a person, participates in this cosmic consciousness. Valéry pursues this point by relating matter, consciousness, and relativity physics to the problem of the person:

> We have here the strangest problem that could ever be proposed, and which others do pose to us: it consists simply in the possibility of other intelligences, in the plurality of the singular, in the co-existence of durations which are independent of one another,— tot capita, tot tempora,—a problem quite similar to the physical problem of relativity, but incomparably more difficult.[21]

The admission of the conscious man that there are other men who also participate in consciousness is difficult because it means, as the text above suggests, the coexistence of independent psychological durations based on existence of independent individuals. Yet all of this is held together in the single continuum of the relativity schema where energy can be matter, and where matter exists at the limit of consciousness. Perhaps this finds expression in the fact that consciousness and matter are but modalities of a single force, energy itself.

Monsieur Teste is precisely an individual who wants to discover the structure of his own consciousness. He wants to be a purely transparent individual, a mirror of pure consciousness. In this way he would be both perfect receiver and the source of all reflections. To this pure state of consciousness Monsieur Teste aspires. He wishes to be "the glass man":

> My vision is so clear, my perception so pure, my knowledge so awkwardly complete, my representative power so unfettered and precise and my understanding so perfect that I can enter myself from the extremities of the earth and reach my silent word; and rising from the formless *thing* that is the object of the search I follow myself along known fibers and ordered centers, I answer myself, I reflect and resonate myself, I tremble before the infinity of mirrors —I am made of glass.[22]

"The glass man" finds its echoes in other writings of Paul Valéry. There are many such resonances of this same kind of self-consciousness in *La Jeune Parque,* finished in 1917. For instance, the reader finds this remarkable parallel to the above quotation in *La Jeune Parque:*

I saw me seeing myself, and glance upon glance
Shed its golden light, serpentine, deep into my innermost forests.[23]

In Monsieur Teste's attempt to understand his individuality he ironically transcends his personality and almost becomes an infinity of mirrors which reflect the light of consciousness. Through this prism myriad colors of the world of objects and persons are refracted. Man's center is found everywhere but nowhere. He has no name, he is simply the mysterious eye, the finite witness to an infinite act:

> Conscious—Teste, Testis.
> This implies an "eternal" observer whose role is limited to repeating and demonstrating the system in which the *I* is the instantaneous part that believes it is the Whole. The I could never come into play if it did not believe it was—the whole.[24]

The reflective person constantly becomes aware of the dreamlike nature of himself and of the world. For these reasons, the metaphor of *La Jeune Parque* waking from her dreamlike state at the edge of the reflecting sea is another image of the same range of possibilities. These possibilities are what constitute the identity of a person. Man realizes that he is but a single reflection of one of the infinite ranges of possibilities. When consciousness disappears, however, then he is condemned to physical death. He realizes that the self has gone full circle. "It is a matter of going from zero to zero. And that is life.—From the unconscious and insensible to the unconscious and insensible."[25] Monsieur Teste comes to his end when consciousness ends. He is a certain manner of being. His marks a personal, particular mode of existence. Although there may be an infinite number of dimensions of which human consciousness is but a single reflection, the totality of these possible dimensions remains eternally hidden even to the purified existence of consciousness:

> M. Teste said to me:
> —Good-bye. Soon . . . a certain way of seeing . . . will be over . . . In a little while, perhaps, before the end comes, I will experience this important moment—and perhaps I will grasp myself whole and entire in one terrible split-second.—But this can never be . . . Here ends the intellect's journey. Funeral march of the mind.[26]

The demon of possibility, Monsieur Teste is the dreamlike goal which seeks to obliterate everything but consciousness to study what is intrinsically personal. As consciousness ends so does Monsieur Teste and his witness to others. Ironically for Monsieur Teste, while he seeks what is uniquely his consciousness, he finds that the relationship between individuals is not distinction, but identity. He illustrates the truth that man is identified with all other men to the extent that he and they participate in and have self-consciousness. He finds that consciousness becomes a prism for his possible existences with others. The study of the structure of consciousness allows man to see how much he is like other men. Monsieur Teste thought that he could begin by finding himself, by cutting himself off from others. His wife recalls that as his witness, he spoke to her as an object, regarding her just as he did everything else outside of his consciousness.[27] Through his experiences Monsieur Teste demonstrates that consciousness and the I cannot be completely identified. Man alone in what originally appears uniquely his, his consciousness, marks an incomplete but fundamental attempt at self-definition.[28]

## MURPHY AND HIS SUCCESSORS— SAMUEL BECKETT

A humorous yet sympathetic reflection of the intense Monsieur Teste's conscious mode of life is the homeless Murphy of Samuel Beckett. Like his brother "heroes" in the Beckett canon, Murphy is persistent in his search for home, sighing, "All life is but a wandering to find home."[29] These "heroes" see their journey homeward as the source of self-definition. The routes that the characters take in the Beckett canon are varied, but all of them embark on some kind of journey while wondering who they are. Murphy's anguish that all life is but a wandering to find home calls forth resonances in *Watt, Molloy, Malone,* and *The Unnamable.* During their labyrinthine search, these self-enclosed heroes begin to face the problem that the protagonist in Robbe-Grillet's *Dans le labyrinthe* experiences; that is, that the searcher and the country to be explored are one. A brief description of the journeys of Beckett's lonely men may perhaps bring about a better understanding of the isolated Murphy.

In the second novel of Samuel Beckett, *Watt,* the reader finds a hero who seems to be on a journey to find the meaning of who he is in terms of a cosmos which challenges his understanding. As a servant in a house of Mr. Knott, Watt cannot pierce his master's mystery. In fact, the whole of Mr. Knott's character and the universe surrounding him is shrouded in the enigma of nothingness. Although the novel has been treated as having many metaphysical implications, the problem of identity in Watt's journey is also significant. Watt in fragmented and parodic statements manifests his frustrated pilgrimage in understanding Knott's universe as it relates to himself: "Of nought. To the source. To the teacher. To the temple. To him I brought. This emptied heart. These emptied hands. This mind ignoring. This body homeless. To love him my little reviled. My little rejected to have him. My little to learn him forgot. Abandoned my little to find him."[30]

As his alter-ego Mr. Knott actually becomes a mirror for Watt himself and is comically spoken of in inverted mirror language. "Deen did taw? Tonk. Tog da taw? Tonk. Luf puk saw? Hap! Deen did tub? Ton sparp. Tog da tub? Ton wonk."[31]

Some critics have seen the betrayal of language in the super-refined rationalizations and intellectualizations of Watt's language as a response to logical positivism.[32] Yet, the novel eludes metaphysics in its comic portrayal of a man in search of self understanding.

*Molloy,* the first novel of the trilogy, also depicts a "hero" in search. The narration in the novel is in the first person, as it is in the other novels of the trilogy. The hero here, however, is even more handicapped in his search than Murphy or Watt. At least Murphy and Watt could walk, whereas the crippled Molloy could only sit motionless writing stories. Helpless in his mother's room, he recounts how he happens to be there. The first part of his tale narrates his encounter with two men in the woods, his escape from them, and his insatiable desire to find his mother. Somehow, his mother is the answer to his quest, a fundamental psychological doctrine on identity: "I resolved to go and see my mother. I needed, before I could resolve to go and see that woman, reasons of an urgent nature . . . and I seized with a trembling at the mere idea of being hindered from going there, I mean to my mother, there and then."[33] Molloy, needing crutches which he attaches to his bicycle, is obsessed with finding his mother and at the same time with the question of who he is: "I had forgotten who I was (excusably) and spoken of myself as I would have of another, if I had been compelled to speak of another. Yes, it sometimes happens and will sometimes happen again that I forget who I am and strut before my eyes, like a stranger."[34]

Here the I of the narrator seems to forget that he is Molloy, momentarily. His self-consciously pretentious language illustrates his frustration. For after a night in a ditch, poor Molloy finds himself in his mother's room only to discover her absent. While Molloy needs to find his mother to tell him who he is, it is only fitting that someone should be looking for Molloy for the same reasons.

The second part of the novel is, therefore, narrated by another I, Moran, who must track down Molloy. Why? He doesn't know. How could sad Molloy know since he can no longer even recognize himself: "Physically speaking it seemed to me I was becoming rapidly unrecognizable. And when I passed my hands over my face, in a characteristic and now more than ever pardonable gesture, the face my hands felt was not my face any more, and the hands my face felt were my hands no longer."[35] Just as Watt finds nothing in Mr. Knott's house, and Molloy finds only himself in his mother's room, Moran parallels his predecessors in reaching the end of his quest in vain.

Malone, the hero of the second novel of the trilogy, while dying is also "journeying." His task is to await death by distracting himself with stories which are punctuated intermittently by self-analysis. Unfortunately, Malone is so crippled that the tool of his journey, his pencil, keeps slipping from him. While Murphy finds pleasure living in his mind, Malone finds it agonizing. At the end of the novel, one of his characters, Lemuel, starts to kill all of the other characters with his hatchet. The "bloody" scene continues as Lemuel's hatchet becomes a hammer, then a stick, and finally a pencil. The deflation episode mirrors the situation of Malone, who while dying kills his characters, and his fragments of self, with a pencil.

The I continues in the third novel of the trilogy, *The Unnamable,* with merely a voice. As a very articulate search for self, this novel receives a separate treatment in a later chapter. There is, however, the very persistent quest for a name, a defined self, which seems to represent the key to the problem of identity. The I of this novel appears to be the result and heir of the problems which his previous fictions foisted upon him. These fictions which are either his creations or possible names for himself almost made him forget that the object of his search was himself.

Murphy, like his successors, is a lonely man. Murphy, though, prefers it that way. Like Monsieur Teste, Murphy tries to ignore the outside world to discover his real I. Like his French friend, Murphy not only believes in the mind, in the head, but wants to make his consciousness the limit of his world. Some readers, following the critic Mintz, claim that there is a correspondence between Beckett's doctrine of the inner life and Murphy.[36]

Suggesting that Samuel Beckett became very fascinated with the dualist idea of the universe and of the body and the mind, Mintz sees in

Beckett's *Murphy* and his other novels the disintegration of the hero as a sign of the breakdown of the body as the machine or the bicycle upon which the mind rides. He believes that the book is inexplicable without referring to Descartes, Geulincx, and Malebranche: "As used in the novel, the doctrine is modified in one important respect; otherwise it is clearly traceable to its source, and so carefully is it woven into the fabric of the book that *Murphy* is inexplicable except by reference to it."[37] Regardless of the extent to which Samuel Beckett finds the dualistic philosophers intriguing, *Murphy* is intelligible, I believe, without reading these philosophers. If, as Mintz suggests, *Murphy* is a very successful novel of ideas, it is more importantly a successfully comic novel of someone seeking in ceaseless frustration to find himself by forgetting the outside world. It is obvious that this ignoring of the outside world, of the body, of material things, and concentrating on the workings of the mind involves a dualism. Yet, it is a dualism which is no more elusive than the fact that man has since the dawn of history been called a composite of body and soul, body and mind. How Descartes differs from Aristotle, Geulincx from Descartes, and Malebranche from all of them, is a matter for philosophy and not necessarily always illuminative of a work of art.[38]

The motto of Geulincx, "ubi nihil vales, etiam ibi nihil velis," becomes a guideline of Murphy's existence; that is, his real self is his mind and not his body. A convinced solipsist, Murphy is an ironic character as well. The critics who identify Beckett with Murphy do not see how Beckett, through the novel's form, treats Murphy not only sympathetically but also paradoxically. The irony throughout the whole Beckett canon is very subtle, inextricably bound to the form. Murphy, for instance, ends his life because of a paradox he cannot resolve. While his philosophy, his way of life, is that the mind is everything and the body is nothing, the body and the outside triumph over the mind in Murphy's interaction with Mr. Endon.

Describing the impotent Murphy's flight from his bodily self, the novel begins with the protagonist sitting naked in his rocking chair, fastened to the chair by seven scarves. Almost rocket-like, Murphy is liberated from his base, his body, and is hurled into the voidless space of his mind. For Murphy this life was so pleasurable that the French version adds that it was almost without pain.

> And life in his mind gave him pleasure, such pleasure that pleasure was not the word.[39]

21

Et le genre de vie qu'il menait dans son esprit lui faisait plaisir, un tel plaisir que c'était presque une absence de douleur.

The sights and the sounds of the outside world finally dim as he comes alive in his mind. Before reading little more than two pages of the novel, the reader is directed to section six for a description of Murphy's mind. Apologetically, the narrator presents this humorous description: "Happily we need not concern ourselves with this apparatus as it really was—that would be an extravagance and an impertinence—but solely with what it felt and pictured itself to be" (p. 107). Possessing everything that is found in the universe outside, his mind is a cosmos; his consciousness a world. As a good philosopher, Murphy calls a mental concept or idea that is accompanied by a physical experience actual, and a mental concept not accompanied by a physical experience virtual. Unfortunately only kicks are a part of his actual experience; caresses are only virtual.

The fact that mental and physical experiences do not always seem to follow one another intensifies the dualism already present in Murphy: "Thus Murphy felt himself split in two, a body and a mind. They had intercourse apparently, otherwise he could not have known that they had anything in common" (p. 109).

Murphy recognizes then the fragmentation of his experience and resolves it by retreating to his mind. Since his body cannot act on his mind and his mind cannot act on his body, he treats his mind as the real self. But he is satisfied with the explanation that some outside synchronizer, a surrogate for the God of Geulincx, makes sense of the interrelationship of body and mind: "Perhaps there was, outside space and time, a non-mental non-physical Kick from all eternity, dimly revealed to Murphy in its correlated modes of consciousness and extension, the kick 'in intellectu' and the kick 'in re.' But where then was the supreme Caress?" (p. 109).

Paradise, then, is practically what Murphy makes of his mind. His real self is where pleasure is, where heaven is, where the I exists totally unhindered and untroubled by the body and the world outside. Murphy places himself in the rocker so that he can be liberated from his body and take refuge in the three zones of his mind. These zones become better centers for the real self as they become more distant from the things of the body. In the first zone of the mind, the light zone, physical and mental phenomena follow one another. "Here the kick that the physical Murphy received, the mental Murphy gave" (p. 111). In this place the pleasure is "reprisal and revenge." In the second zone of the mind, the half light, Murphy is not interested in matching physical and mental data; his only concern is the quiet bliss of contemplation. The third zone, the dark, is the place of total freedom. In this zone Murphy is most content; here there is no effort, no desire, nothing in which the body has a part: "Thus as his body set him free more and more in his mind, he took to spending less and less time in the light, spitting at the breakers of the world; and less in the half light, where the choice of bliss introduced an element of effort; and more and more and more in the dark, in the will-lessness, a mote in its absolute freedom" (p. 113).

It is perfectly understandable why Murphy retreats to his mind if it is powerless outside of its own sphere. He understands that he can govern himself, can be independent, only in his mind and therefore wastes no energy in attempting to control the external world. Murphy is really unconcerned about an explanation; he merely accepts the fact that his mind is cut off from his body. Frustrated that he has no power outside of his mind, he tries to forget about the outside world. He brings to mind not only Geulincx's "humana mea conditio penitus independens a me" (my human condition is entirely independent of me), but also his "ubi nihil vales, ibi nihil velis" (where you can do nothing, there you wish for nothing). It seems foolish to Murphy to be concerned about the big world outside. The little world, the world of his mind alone has meaning. This is the reason why he envies the inmates of Magdalen Mental Mercyseat where he finds employment. He envies them because they are free to spend all of their time lost in the freedom of their mind. Only such persons, Murphy is convinced, are true human persons; they have found real happiness in their isolation. In spite of his admiration for the inmates, it is evident that Murphy distorts their groans and pains into meaning what he wants them to mean: "The frequent expressions apparently of pain, rage, despair and in fact all the usual, to which some patients gave vent, suggesting a fly somewhere in the ointment of Microcosmos, Murphy either disregarded or muted to mean what he wanted" (p. 179).

Their condition was a happy one and nothing could change that for Murphy. They had achieved the paradise for which he was searching. Beckett begins this chapter emphasizing the point: "Il est difficile à celui qui vit hors du monde de ne pas rechercher les siens" (p. 156).

One of the most delightful moments in the hospital for Murphy was playing chess with a psychotic named Mr. Endon. Becoming attached to Mr. Endon, Murphy seeks some type of expression and some sort of recognition from him. Humorously and also sympathetically the narrator describes Murphy's inspection of Mr. Endon's eyes: "Approaching his eyes still nearer Murphy could see the red frills of mucus, a large point of suppuration at the root of an upper lash, the filigree of veins like the Lord's prayer on a toenail and in the cornea, horribly reduced, obscured and distorted, his own image. They were all set, Murphy and Mr. Endon, for a butterfly kiss, if that is still the correct expression" (p. 249).

Murphy's search for some recognition in Mr. Endon is actually betraying his commitment to the inner life. He needs Mr. Endon but Mr. Endon can do nothing more than return a distorted image for Murphy. It is this that forces him to confront himself again. Murphy wants to live entirely in his mind and admires Mr. Endon for seemingly being able to do so. Ironically, Murphy's admiration for Endon forces him to want to transcend himself. He rediscovers his need for another person in a man whose response he could not control.

> Kneeling at the bedside, the hair starting in the thick black ridges between his fingers, his lips, nose and forehead almost touching Mr. Endon's, seeing himself stigmatised in those eyes that did not see him, Murphy heard words demanding so strongly to be spoken that he spoke them, right into Mr. Endon's face, Murphy who did not speak at all in the ordinary way unless spoken to, and not always even then.

> > "the last at last seen of him
> > himself unseen by him
> > and of himself." (P. 249)

Not only does the tone reflect the irony with which Beckett treats Murphy's need for the other and his inability to remain within himself but also the sad fact that Endon could not return anything to Murphy: "The revelation between Mr. Murphy and Mr. Endon could not have been better summed up than by the former's sorrow at seeing himself in the latter's immunity from seeing anything but himself" (p. 258).

Murphy finds that he needs more than his own distorted reflection in Endon's eye; he needs the recognition and response of another person. Mr. Endon, like Mr. Knott in *Watt* and Monsieur Teste, also becomes a mirror without the ability of relational response for the viewer, leaving both in a Narcissus type limbo. A true psychotic, Mr. Endon is someone really caught and imprisoned within himself, for he could not relate to

Murphy. Yet, if it is a paradise for Mr. Endon to live in his mind and to ignore everyone outside, it is also a sorrow for Murphy to be a part of that outside. Perhaps this is a lesson that the solipsist, Murphy, learns before his death : that the macrocosm will take its revenge on those who choose to ignore it.

The relationship of Murphy to his mind and to the external world fashions the plot of the novel. He is as separated from society as his mind is from his body. He does not trouble himself with any kind of work since that would bring him into relationship with society, with the outside, which he cannot order. He tells Celia that he refuses to enter "the jaws of a job."

The only reason Murphy finally does work is for Celia whom he loves or rather whom his body loves. She is a prostitute who, for Murphy, represents union with society and self-transcendence. Since she threatens to leave him unless Murphy starts to work, because she alone makes money and Murphy makes nothing, Murphy takes a job in the Mercyseat hospital at the suggestion of his friend Ticklepenny. Before beginning his work, Murphy consults an astrologist who represents the inscrutable control that Murphy could not exert over himself, other persons, or society.

Murphy sees Celia as a link with society and his body. He, consequently, is ashamed of his relationship with her, since it is against his doctrine of the inner life. "My God, how I hate the charVenus and her sausage and mash sex" (p. 37). While it is his body which loves Celia, not his mind, Murphy has a hard time controlling his body. He is embarrassed over the fact that he had some kind of feeling for Celia. Murphy is ashamed of his relationship with Celia because she is a part of the world which he cannot control. She means a love for which he has no use because he cannot understand it. He cannot understand her because love involves the whole person and not merely the mind.

While Murphy seeks escape from Celia, from society, from the other, and retreats into his own mind for the real world, he eventually faces the challenge of the other with Mr. Endon. Because Murphy ignores the outside and concentrates on his own mind, he can only exist for a time with his doctrine of the inner life. As Monsieur Teste passes from zero to zero, from unconsciousness to unconsciousness, so does Murphy. He ends his life in an ecstasy during which the gas jet in the W.C. goes on.

Murphy represents the search for self in man alone. Within his consciousness in "black absolute freedom" Murphy seeks his real self.

Society, in the form of work or in love for a person, represented by Celia, challenges his doctrine of the inner life and the real self which his mind represents. Murphy, however, seeks himself in vain. It is only after the chess game with Mr. Endon that he sorrowfully speaks about his own obscure, distorted image in Mr. Endon's eye. This realization calls forth the necessity of witness as a complement to consciousness in determining identity. The need for the other in establishing identity and self-definition emerges as Murphy's search is terminated. This need for the other becomes rather significant in the pair-relationships in *Waiting for Godot, Endgame, Watt,* and the *Trilogy.* The temptation to solipsism is continually present in the works after *Murphy;* yet each of the pair reaffirms that he cannot go on without the other as Gogo and Didi suggest.

Herein lies the difficulty with the critical approach that would ascribe Murphy's doctrine to Beckett himself. Beckett is treating sympathetically and humorously the story of a man committed to the search for himself within his own mind who finds that this is impossible. Neither Murphy nor Beckett are faithful to their "master," Geulincx, and, consequently, project an artistic meaning beyond the philosophical doctrines of either the author or the character. Even in *The Unnamable*— in fact, throughout Beckett's works—the search for the I continues in that same sympathetic, ironic, and parodic tone. The tone in *The Unnamable* changes and becomes even more parodic and intense in the search for a name conducted by an even more obscure ego. The I in his search for meaning and a name in *The Unnamable* is inextricably wedded to words and the function of words in the quest for the self; this aspect of the quest will be discussed more fully in a later chapter.

Murphy, like Monsieur Teste, finds that consciousness as "the real self" has definite limits. Murphy dies and Monsieur Teste experiences a metaphorical death when consciousness is at its zero point and sleep takes over. The death of each is a very individual thing, marked by the mind's end and the cessation of consciousness. To what extent man finds himself within himself is a difficult question. Murphy and Monsieur Teste are dedicated to the principle that life in the mind is the real world. They indicate the real attraction and significance for the individual of the journey within. They also indicate, ironically, the importance and need for the individual to journey outside to the other, to society.

Through self-study Monsieur Teste begins to understand the structure of his own consciousness and how much he is related and identified with all men who possess consciousness. Murphy, in retreating to his own mind, sees that it is only half an existence when he meets Mr. Endon with whom he wishes to relate. Both characters, Murphy and Teste, are sympathetic because they are committed to an ideal which has an attraction for men since it reveals a truth about the self and since it is one way to deal with man's impotency in society. Through the journey inward, Monsieur Teste and Leonardo da Vinci are seen in their conscious activity as identifiable. Through his journey inward and his admiration for the paradigm of this journey in Mr. Endon, Murphy learns that he too cannot find himself totally within himself. The journey inward strangely and ironically reveals how much men are alike and identified and how much they need one another in being able to find a more secure center in themselves. Both Murphy and Monsieur Teste reveal that man alone is only half man, and that his existence, his consciousness, seeks by its own existence a participation in the conscious awareness of others.

The fact that man cannot find his total identity within himself may seem rather obvious, but even partial self-identification is important. A doctrine of total solipsism leads to an eventual confrontation with a Mr. Endon; but a life of no journey inward ignores aspects of the self which are not always easily recoverable. The search for self can take all kinds of divergent forms. If a person claims that what is really his and uniquely his is his own mind, his own consciousness, the search for the self is a corollary and a necessity to the analysis of one's mind. If self-definition rests in distinction more than in identity then Murphy and Monsieur Teste are right in their journey; they do discover themselves as individuals in their search. If, however, self-definition resides more in relations, then their journey is incomplete. The likable Murphy and the awesome Teste see in some way that their own consciousness reveals them to be more alike.

Eventually, then, all the mirror images of the protagonists, Knott of Watt, Mr. Endon of Murphy, *homme de verre* of Monsieur Teste, leave their subjects eager for a response beyond that of mere reflection and inverted images. They echo in some way the cry of Narcissus to be delivered from himself and call forth the need for a real relation to others. The relation to the other permits the individual who begins to define himself by opposition to discover that he can continue only by identification and dialogue with others on his pilgrimage to the real "me."

## 2 / THE OTHER AND IDENTITY: THE COUPLES

## OF SAMUEL BECKETT

The role of other people in helping to define the self has been treated a great deal since the contributions of Martin Buber. Man alone cannot find the "real me." He needs the experience which comes from relationships with other people, with "thous." That through a "Thou" a man becomes an "I" is Buber's rather familiar thesis.[1] The importance of the recognition by the "I" that there is a "thou" is found in the fact that the relationship between "I" and "thou" allows the individual to be transformed into a person. Monsieur Teste and Murphy discover in their isolation that being alone allows only one aspect of the self to emerge. They never manage to transcend the category of individual. Their relationship is one which is characteristic of the "I-it" relationship in Buber's terms. In this relationship the I makes its appearance as individuality and is aware of itself as a subject who experiences and uses. In the relationship which is called "I-thou," the I emerges as a person who is conscious of itself as subjectivity. Individuality, in other words, is formed in opposition to or in differentiation from other individualities. A person is formed according to Buber not by opposition but by relationship: "A person makes his appearance by entering into relations with other persons."[2] Monsieur Teste and Murphy do recognize their need for other people as Roquentin seems to while looking at his face in the mirror and as Narcissus does in wishing that he might find another instead of himself in the pool. Although the couples of Samuel Beckett present an antiheroic and fragmented form of the I-Thou relationship, they manage to achieve a rather sophisti-

28

cated form of personhood by their recognition of the other. Their need for the other and its value in discovering a new self is tenaciously clung to.

The heroes of Samuel Beckett are consistently observed as solitary individuals, nevertheless, the couple is one of the most commonly used devices in his writings. The couple and the pair are found in all areas of the Beckett canon. The symbol transcends genres and takes on prismatic significance as the style and the genres change. Although it is true that the impotent heroes of Beckett appear as solitary, their very aloneness suggests the extent to which they need the other.

Many writers could be used as a basis for an exploration of the search for identity as found in a relationship to the other. Gabriel Marcel is one such philosopher and playwright. In an essay entitled "The Drama of the Soul in Exile," Gabriel Marcel stresses the fact that the soul in exile is the man who, as a stranger to himself, has lost his way.[3] This man can find himself only with others. It is only through the realization that he is not alone that he can find his path again. Christiane in Marcel's *Le Monde cassé* tells her husband that they are not alone, that no one is because there is a communion of sinners as well as of saints.[4] This need for the other then is inevitable. It is as important in the reduced characters of Beckett as it is in the sophisticated personages of Marcel. In Samuel Beckett the couples do not form a community of saints or sinners but rather a community of vagabonds.

The works of Samuel Beckett, consequently, provide a valuable insight, since the disintegration of syntax often mirrors the fragmentation of the "hero." The hero, whether simply a body whose physical situation has diminished or just a voice, is always in a suggested or real relationship to another. The remnant of a voice in the I who is related to others always finds that it is through this relationship that the I is capable of being I. From an early poem to *How It Is* the pieces of identity which are associated with the individual imply and call forth the other for self-identification.

In "Cascando" (1936), Beckett articulates the tension between being alone and the need for the other in a way which will be recalled again and again in his novels and plays:

2.

saying again
if you do not teach me I shall not learn

29

saying again there is a last
even of last times
last times of begging
last times of loving
of knowing not knowing pretending
a last even of last times of saying
if you do not love me I shall not be loved
If I do not love you I shall not love

the churn of stale words in the heart again
love love love thud of the old plunger
pestling the unalterable
whey of words

terrified again
of not loving
of loving and not you
of being loved and not by you
of knowing not knowing pretending
pretending

I and all the others that will love you
if they love you

3.

unless they love you[5]

The conflict between the aloneness of the individual and his need for communication is used as a contrapuntal theme or, better, the base of the chord in all of Beckett's writings. The couples and pairs in his plays, however, are probably the best examples of this conflict in the need for the other. In *Waiting for Godot* there are, for instance, Vladimir and Estragon or Gogo and Didi, the boy and his brother, Pozzo and Lucky, and even the two thieves. The couples are important in that they provide a witness basis for identity. Since Samuel Beckett in all of this is saying more than that man is basically solitary, the need for the other has a more subtle point. For the awarenness of the existence of someone other permits one to say I to oneself. Consequently, each person in the pair reinforces the personality of the other.

In *Waiting for Godot* the tension between being alone and the need for the other is sadly expressed by Estragon at the end of the first act. He tells Vladimir that perhaps they would have been better off alone:

> ESTRAGON : Wait! (*He moves away from Vladimir.*)
> I sometimes wonder if we wouldn't have been better off alone, each one for himself. (*He crosses the stage and sits down on the mound.*) We weren't made for the same road.
> VLADIMIR : (*without anger*) It's not certain.
> ESTRAGON : No, nothing is certain.[6]

The play, composed of two acts, ends on the same note, uncertainty about the fact that they are better off together. In fact, at the end of the second act, Estragon repeats the same ambiguity in their relationship:

> ESTRAGON : I can't go on like this.
> VLADIMIR : That's what you think.
> ESTRAGON : If we parted? That might be better for us.[7]

At the time that the play ends Vladimir and Estragon are leaving together. One says "Shall we go?" The other responds "Yes, let's go." But the stage directions are very significant at the end of both acts, "They do not move." In other words, they are there together, waiting for Godot who represents some transcendental experience that never comes; yet their hope continues. They cannot wait alone because without the other to whom "you" can be said, without the relationship of the other, the waiting has no witness. Vladimir and Gogo need one another to witness and to identify one another while they are waiting.

Both a statement about this need and a humorous exemplification of it are apparent in their attempt at embracing. After a rhythmic exchange of insults such as "Moron!" "Vermin!" and so forth, they move apart from one another, face each other, move apart again, and as the stage direction says:

> (*They embrace. They separate. Silence.*)
> VLADIMIR : How time flies when one has fun![8]

It is almost as if their waiting together, the embracing, are parodies of passing the time as well as of inevitable interactions. While their tricks are often ludicrous, Gogo and Didi are very intuitively aware of the importance that the witness of the other provides:

> VLADIMIR: Or for night to fall. (*Pause.*) We have kept our appoint-
> ment and that's an end to that. We are not saints, but we have
> kept our appointment. How many people can boast as much ?[9]

It is particularly through this declaration that the play takes on a hope which is beyond despair. Regardless of how impotent and frustrating their hope is, they manage to survive together.

There are more subtle examples of the pair in *Waiting for Godot*. The boy who comes to announce Mr. Godot's delay claims that he has a brother. Both he and his brother work for Godot. He tells Vladimir that he minds the goats while his brother, who minds the sheep, is beaten by Godot. The other example in the play is Pozzo and Lucky. Pozzo enters driving Lucky onto the stage. Connected to one another by a rope and echoing the play on words that Vladimir and Estragon exchange in their own relationship about being tied, Pozzo and Lucky enter as torturer and victim. The other pair mentioned but not capable of stage presence are the Good Thief and the Bad Thief, one of whom receives eternal punishment, the other eternal happiness. All of these pairs complement one another to the extent that their punishments and status are gratuitous, one is the opposite of the other: one of the boys is beaten, the other is not; one of the thieves is saved, the other is damned; Gogo has stinking feet and Vladimir has stinking breath. Each witnesses the other's waiting, the other's suffering, the other's privation; but more important, without the witness value of the other, there would be no one for whom Gogo and Didi could have names. Their names only come from the fact that there is another from whom they are distinguished.

*Endgame* also uses doubles. Clov and Hamm as well as Nagg and Nell complete one another in their tortured existence. Hamm expresses a very profound aspect of the double when he says: "It's we are obliged to each other."[10] After being thanked for his services, Clov responds that he is obliged to Hamm; but Hamm refuses to express it in one-sided terms. He claims that they owe each other their existence. Hamm also seems to describe their life together as a game echoing the "fun" that Gogo and Didi have while they try to pass the time. They also complement one another in their suffering. Hamm cannot stand up and is blind; Clov cannot sit down. Their need for one another is so intense that they are really aspects of each other's partial existence. Yet they torment one another in their games. Hamm, for instance, cries out for his dog while Clov violently beats him over the head with the dog. They are trying to end their torment of one another, but if their torment ends, their existence and identity also end. At the end of the play after Clov has left, Hamm says: "Well, there we are, there I am, that's enough."[11] The play, like *Waiting for Godot,* is cyclical in its structure. It ends with Hamm sitting in his chair covered with a handkerchief almost as if he is waiting for Clov to return to take off the handkerchief again. While the play opens with both Hamm and Clov on the stage, it ends with Hamm alone on the stage. Yet Hamm in the final tableau suggests the presence of Clov on stage.

Moreover, while Hamm and Clov are suffering together, on the stage in two ashcans are Nell and Nagg who, in their agony, unsuccessfully try to communicate with one another. When Hamm asks how Nagg is, whether he is even alive, Clov looks into the can and sees him crying. Clov's response again expresses the joyless existence:

> HAMM: Then he's living.
> (*Pause*)
> Did you ever have an instant of happiness?
> CLOV: Not to my knowledge.
> (*Pause*)[12]

Nell and Nagg are mirror reflections of the suffering of Hamm and Clov. This really is the end of all games by means of which people try to idle away their hours of suffering together. They do, however, even in the midst of their mutual torment, provide an answer. For in the midst of a very timeworn cosmos they are the lone survivors of life. This play ends, as *Waiting for Godot* does, with a hope which is never really extinguished. For outside of the window, Clov sees a little boy whom he tells Hamm about: "If he exists he'll die there or he'll come here. And if he doesn't . . ."[13] Hamm continues by saying that he doesn't need Clov anymore. The boy may represent the surrogate of Clov. If he does exist he will be a witness; if he doesn't and is merely the invention of Clov, Clov must remain. Hamm believes in the boy, as he says: "It's the end, Clov, we've come to the end. I don't need you any more."[14] After this Clov makes his final exit and Hamm is provided with the final witness, that of the audience acting as a group in its provisionary role as the other double.

*Happy Days* has a single couple in it, Winnie and Willie. Their search for communication, for complementary fulfillment, is obstructed by the fact that Winnie is up to her waist in a mound and Willie must climb up the mound to relate. They do relate at the end in a parody of communication as Winnie sings a song of happy days:

Win! (*Pause.*) Oh this *is* a happy day, this will have been another happy day! (*Pause.*) After all. (*Pause.*) So far.

(*Pause. She hums tentatively beginning a song, then sings softly, musical-box tone.*)

Though I say not
What I may not
Let you hear,
Yet the swaying
Dance is saying,
Love me dear!
Every touch of fingers,
Tells me what I know,
Says for you,
It's true, it's true,
You love me so![15]

The novels, too, use the symbol of the couple. In the discussion of *Watt,* for instance, it has already been observed that without Watt's witness Mr. Knott ceases to exist. Murphy, too, needs someone in spite of his rejection of Celia and society. In fact, only after Murphy realizes that he is not a part of the consciousness of Mr. Endon, a witness to his existence, does Murphy end his life. The importance of the other continues in the *Trilogy.* Molloy is looking for his mother; Moran is looking for Molloy; and Malone, the storyteller, is the creator and destroyer of his many witnesses, his characters. The importance of the other reaches a new dimension in *The Unnamable.* The I of the Unnamable relates in succession to several others: Basil becomes Mahood, Mahood becomes Worm. The I detests all of these yet at the same time he needs them. Sometimes they, "these others," confuse him by making him think they are he; but he knows that he can never begin to define himself, have a story, try a life, without the witness of the other. No matter how dominant the voice of the other becomes, the I knows that it is not his.

This need for the other continues to grow until infinite resonances are suggested. In part one of the novel *How It Is,* the I begins his journey through the mud rejecting the voices of the others who once made him think that their voices were his. These former voices came from within the I and are previous bearers of his personality: "in me that were without when the panting stops scraps of an ancient voice in me not mine.[16] Pim, the goal of his search, is unlike the masks of his other life. Pim's voice comes from outside; the Unnamable's voices were from within. In fact, the I is surprised when he hears him, for instead of speaking or telling stories, as the others had done, Pim sings. The I is surprised yet he is glad to hear a human voice: "no doubt that only one way of being where I was namely my way song quite out of the question."[17] He even begins to enjoy Pim's song. Here Pim seems to be more than a cause of self-identification for the I; he is almost a source for transcending the self in "a moment of beauty." Richard Coe observes that Pim represents the promise of human contact, the goal of human contact, making the nauseating journey worthwhile.[18] The meeting of the I and Pim present a grotesque parody of communication. Lying side by side in the mud, Pim and the I communicate:

> my right hand seeks his lips let us try and see this pretty movement more clearly its conclusion at least

> the hand approaches under the mud comes up at a venture the index encounters the mouth it's vague it's well judged the thumb the cheek somewhere something wrong. . .

> I can't make out the words the mud muffles or perhaps a foreign tongue perhaps he's singing a lied in the original perhaps a foreigner.[19]

Part one traces how it was before Pim, part two tells how it was with Pim, and part three narrates how it was after Pim. Here, in part three of *How It Is,* the use of the couple reaches its highest scale of overtones: "at the instant I reach Pim another reaches Bem we are regulated thus our justice wills it thus fifty thousand couples again at the same instant the same everywhere."[20] The couples, like Hamm and Clov and Pim and I, torment one another; they are mutual victims and tormentors: "I frequent number 4 and number 2 in my quality of victim and tormentor respectively and number 2 and number 4 frequent number 3 in their quality of tormentor and victim respectively."[21] This is another form of the parody in which the couples need one another to torment one another in their journey toward identification. Yet, even after meeting Pim and drawing out the possibilities of couples to infinity, the I still wonders what his name is: "and this business of a procession no answer this business of a procession yes never any procession no nor any journey no never any Pim no nor any Bom no never anyone no only me no answer only me yes so that was true yes it was true about me yes and what's my name no answer WHAT'S MY NAME screams good."[22] The yeses and the noes of this section alternate in the verses. One verse is predominantly a "yes"; another a "no." The tension between affirmation and negation expresses the state in which the individual person in the couple finds himself related. These distortions and exaggerations are the necessary ingredients of humor, pointing up the essential ambivalence in human relationships.

The I of *How It Is* seems to be the same voice of the *Trilogy* continuing his question from one relationship to another. The I of the novels is pursuing his journey together, alone, together again; the I relates to Molloy, Malone, Basil, Worm, Mahood, Pim, and others. This need almost appears invincible because without the other the I has no one whose opposition to self helps define the self. As soon as the I says: "He is not Murphy," for example, he moves on to someone else looking for a positive answer to the question of his identity rather than merely the negative "I am not he." Although each relationship for a time proves the self's unique and distinct existence, it still leaves him restlessly searching alone.

While the quest for identity, the quest for the meaning of the I through the relationship to the other is the same, the search takes on different shifts of tone and mood in the different genres. For instance, Hamm's speech in *Endgame* parallels in significance the last ramblings of the I in *The Unnamable*. Hamm says, "The end is in the beginning and yet you go on."[23] The I in *The Unnamable* cries, "You must go on, that's all I know . . . perhaps they have carried me to the threshold of my story."[24] Both Hamm and the I of *The Unnamable* are convinced that the end contains the beginning and they are both cyclical. They are both concerned with the tension between silence and words. Silence means aloneness to Hamm as well as to the I of *The Unnamable*. Hamm says, "There I'll be, in the old shelter, alone against the silence."[25] The Unnamable stutters, "It will be I, it will be the silence, where I am, I don't know."[26] Both the I of *The Unnamable* and Hamm are also worried about the words that make up their story. Hamm says, "Perhaps I could go on with my story, end it and begin another."[27] The Unnamable insists, ''Perhaps they have carried me to the threshold of my story, before the door that opens on my story.''[28] Hamm also suggests the method of journey or procession that the I of *How It Is* uses: ''Dig my nails into the cracks and drag myself forward with my fingers.''[29] While the I of the novels has the reader become his double at the end, Hamm has, in addition to the audience as a double, Clov, to whom he is addressing these lines. Clov, however, does not hear them because he has left and the audience understands that his comments are a description of his past life with Clov.

There are differences between the vagabonds of the novels and those of the plays. Out of necessity the characters in the play have been given faces, bodies, and masks that are concretized on the stage. The characters in the novels do not have to be that whole. While the quest and their relationship to the other might involve the same meaning, the characters in the novel can be given a voice without a body. Stage characters who are spoken about and waited for but never manage to appear represent reduced existences. In the novel the voice of the reduced character is even determined by the form in which the print falls on the page. This is particularly true when the reader compares the form of the verse style of *How It Is* to the block style of *The Unnamable*. *How It Is* almost conveys the mode of a play because of tone and voice changes in its versification. While the physical qualities of the character may be more specific and determined in the play, the voice of the I can be made piercing in the novel. For example, the I in *How It Is* knows that he is the same I who was before he met Pim, while he was with Pim, and after Pim. The important conclusion that can be drawn from the I's encounter with Pim is that he has recognized Pim as the other and still can say ''I'' to self. The I and the you of the personages on stage are necessarily separate and distinct. They remain, however, in their identities relational rather than oppositional. Hamm understands this when he tells Clov, ''It's we are obliged to each other.''[30]

Identity, then, in the couple or double is determined by relationships. Regardless of how deprived the pair are and how tormented they are, they are still obliged to each other. The other provides them with the ability to say you. Actually, even if everyone and everything else is abandoned, there is still a part of self that one can say ''I'' to, and this through a meeting with the other. Pim causes the I to realize, after he has met him and abandoned him, that the I is still the same I who was before and with Pim.

The significance of the couple in Samuel Beckett is parodic and unromantic and yet very important. The other is the hope, the goal of communication, the reason that one can say I to self, the witness of the other's pain and torment. People ''are obliged to one another'' to define themselves. They are confused at times by the other who makes the I forget himself as in *The Unnamable.* Yet, the I can continue to insist that he is not those others, rather that he is himself because he still has that part of his personality which remains constant even after the contact with the other. *Endgame* and *Waiting for Godot,* suggest that the couples never end but are drawn out in time as *How It Is* draws them out in number and geometry. They form both in time and in space the source from which there is a second person to whom the first is related as a distinct and continuing existence. The other person allows the self to overcome its individuality and become a person.

Although Buber would not find these solitary wretches of Beckett exactly inspiring examples, they have even in their vagabond state recognized the goal of personhood. They have gone beyond the solitary witness of consciousness which Teste and Murphy evidence, and in their mutual torment have found a way to survive together. In exchangeable roles of victim and torturer, the pairs always find the right ditch, tree, or mound to provide them with the opportunity to overcome total aloneness and form the human comedy of a community of vagabonds.[31] They still have trouble with name words and pronouns, which means that the journey to the real self is incomplete. Relationships with other people, pronouns, and words, while necessary ingredients to discovering the self, sometimes foist pseudo identity on the searcher in the form of personae or roles. Words and other people can construct masks and covers to the self, obstacles which must be confronted in the journey. Since other people imply dialogue and language as well as possible sources for role exchanges, these two realities of experience are explored in separate chapters, one on words and the self, and one on masks.

# 3 / MYTH AND THE SELF

The word, the story, and the self are parts of a larger area in which identity is often sought; that is, the area of myth and its relationship to language. Although many examples and forms from modern literature could be explored from this perspective, I would like to treat particularly James Joyce, William Faulkner, and Samuel Beckett. While these novelists use language to form different mythical structures, they complement one another prismatically in their statements on the self.

Myth in recent times has been discussed anthropologically by Claude Lévi-Strauss, philosophically by Ernst Cassirer, and in literary categories by Northrop Frye. These scientifically different approaches all converge at one point: they agree that the language of myth and the language of self are identical. Before the discussion of the novels there will be a brief treatment of the nature of myth, its relationship to language, and its relevance to the meaning of self. Since myth is also profoundly relevant to the discussion on masks as well as to the sections on labyrinths, this outline will serve as an introduction to chapter 4 and chapter 5 as well.

Claude Lévi-Strauss claims that myth is language and at the same time different from language.[1] What gives myth its value is its ability to explain past, present, and future. For this reason, Lévi-Strauss concludes: "Myth is language, functioning on an especially high level where meaning succeeds practically at "taking off" from the linguistic ground on which it keeps on rolling."[2]

Myth as language has to be told to be known. An early meaning of myth in the Greek, muthos, means word or story. Mythical story, according to Lévi-Strauss, can be translated: "Myth is the part of language where the formula *traduttore, tradittore* reaches its lowest truth value."[3] Consequently, Lévi-Strauss places myth and poetry at opposite ends of a continuum, because he claims that poetry is a kind of speech which cannot be translated except at the cost of real distortion. The constituent units of myth differ from language in that they belong to a more complex order. These constituent units, he claims, consist of a relation: "From this springs a new hypothesis, which constitutes the very core of our argument: The true constituent units of a myth are not the isolated relations but *bundles of such relations,* and it is only as bundles that these relations can be put to use and combined so as to produce meaning."[4]

Myth, moreover, involves a continual process in which contradictions seek mediation. While seeking to overcome a logical contradiction, myth has its own kind of logic, and it is as exacting as that of modern science: "The difference lies, not in the quality of the intellectual process, but in the nature of the things to which it is applied."[5] For Lévi-Strauss, then, mythical thought is characterized by the tendency in man to refuse to accept contradictions as they stand.

Another approach to myth is that given by Mircea Eliade, whose concept is related to that of Malinowski and other functionalists.[6] Eliade's stress is on the religious rather than on the sociological dimension of myth. In his book, *Myth and Reality,* Eliade states that myth should be considered as an absolutely true story that narrates a sacred history within its own cultural milieu.[7] Myth, for him, is never an allegorical interpretation of reality in which the gods are merely personifications of the forces of nature. Myth always deals with a sacred reality: "It narrates a sacred history; it relates an event that took place in primordial Time, the fabled time of the 'beginnings.' In other words, myth tells how, through the deeds of supernatural Beings, a reality came into existence, be it the whole of reality, the Cosmos, or only a fragment of reality."[8]

Considered in this light, myth is always an account of a creation. It relates how something came to be. This creation, in all cases, narrates the breaking in of the transcendent, of the sacred, into the world. Myth, therefore, teaches man primordial stories and relates him in an I-Thou pattern to the sacred and the transcendent. Through a ritual participation in the sacred, man overcomes the contradictions of life. Consequently, man recalls what was done *in illo tempore* for it is through this anamnesis that he faces the world without fear:

Myth assures man that what he is about to do *has already been done,* in other words, it helps him to overcome doubts as to the result of his undertaking. There is no reason to hesitate before setting out on a sea voyage, because the mythical Hero has already made it in a fabulous Time. All that is needed is to follow his example. Similarly, there is no reason to fear settling in an unknown, wild territory, because one knows what one has to do. One has merely to repeat the cosmogonic ritual, whereupon the unknown territory (= "Chaos") is transformed into "Cosmos", becomes an *imago mundi* and hence a ritually legitimized "habitation."[9]

In this sense the myth opens up the world to man and speaks to him through symbols. The world, in a word, reveals itself as a language: "The World is no longer an opaque mass of objects arbitrarily thrown together, it is a living Cosmos, articulated and meaningful. In the last analysis, *the World reveals itself as a language.*"[10] For Eliade, too, then, myth is concerned with the reconciliation of opposites. Through the retelling of the story man participates in the myth. Through an anamnesis he lives the reality of the myth which took place *in illo tempore.*

Ernst Cassirer, the great philosopher of myth, points out that what is significant in the primitive mentality is not logic, but a certain sentiment of life:

> Language and myth are near of kin. In the early stages of human culture their relation is so close and their cooperation so obvious that it is almost impossible to separate the one from the other. They are two different shoots from one and the same root. Whenever we find man we find him in possession of the faculty of speech and under the influence of the myth-making function.[11]

Myth is another way of seeing the world. It is an emotional assertion of man's place in the world that is meaningful to him. It involves a dramatic response to the recognition that man and his cosmos form a solidarity. Mythic time is always present and the myth recreates and represents what took place *in illo tempore:* it actualizes what it tells. It then may provide man with the values and moral codes which justify his mode of living, giving him a stability amid flux and confusion.

Cassirer explains further the relationship of myth to language. Language, the expression of thought, while not hindering scientific thinking, gives preference to another mode of thinking. For although language is the prime tool of reason, it reflects man's myth-making tendency more than his rationalizing ability. Consequently, as the symbolization of thought, language expresses two different modes of thinking: the one involving discursive reason, and the other the creative imagination.[12]

Language is born out of the need for emotional expression. Not merely exclamatory, it seeks to hold the object of feeling instead of communicating the feeling itself. The word, or the name, fixes the object as a permanent point and experience. Consequently, whenever an emotion is evoked it receives a name, whether it is evoked in relationship to lightning, thunder, animal, or what have you. The name endows emotional responses with a unity, permanence, and substantiality, and fixes them in consciousness. The process is not merely nomenclature but the reflection of a deeper process. This process of image-making or imagination is the most universal talent of the human mind, from which evolves all of language.

Beginning with this realization that all thought involves symbolic expression, Cassirer is led to a theory of symbolic forms. He distinguishes four autonomous forms: language, myth, art, and science.[13] In his attempts at discovering the particular way of seeing that is involved in each of the symbolic forms, Cassirer discovers that myth and language are equally related: the power of the spoken word is particularly brought out in a person's name which is never a mere symbol but is rather a part of him and contains the essence of his being:

> The essential identity between the word and what it denotes becomes even more patently evident if we look at it not from the objective standpoint, but from a subjective angle. For even a person's ego, his very self and personality, is indissolubly linked, in mythic thinking, with his name. Here the name is never a mere symbol, but is part of the personal property of its bearer; property which must be carefully protected, and the use of which is exclusively and jealously reserved to him.[14]

Since the use of a person's name calls that person into being, and makes him present, the process of the word is not merely wedded to conscious experience but consumed by it: "Whatever has been fixed by a name, henceforth is not only real, but is Reality. The potential between "symbol" and "meaning" is resolved; in place of a more or less adequate "expression," we find a relation of identity, of complete congruence between "image" and "object," between the name and the thing."[15]

Thus the word becomes the great revealer of reality. The word is able to unveil a world that would be otherwise hidden from man. It is through the word and through language that man makes his first steps toward self-transcendence. "Indeed, it is the Word, it is language, that really reveals to man that world which is closer to him than any world of natural objects and touches his weal and woe more directly than physical nature. For it is language that makes his existence in a *community* possible; and only in society, in relation to a "Thee," can his subjectivity assert itself as a 'Me.' "[16]

Language, then, becomes the very basis for relational activity between individuals. Consequently, language is both the tool of discursive reason and the expression of the mythic mind. It operates on two distinct levels:

> Language moves in the middle kingdom between the "indefinite" and the "infinite"; it transforms the indeterminate into a determinate idea, and then holds it within the sphere of finite determinations. So there are, in the realm of mythic and religious conception, "ineffables" of different order, one of which represents the lower limit of verbal expression, the other the upper limit; but between these bounds, which are drawn by the very nature of verbal expression, language can move with perfect freedom, and exhibit all the wealth and concrete exemplification of its creative power.[17]

Cassirer goes on to show how the myth-making mind exhibits a real consciousness of the relationship between its results and the phenomena of language. This characteristic is expressed not in logical terms but in images. The lower limits of language express the momentary deities. The upper limit expresses the infinite, static, timeless absolute. Through the opposition of these two views mythical thought gives birth to the rational discursive mode of self-expression. Rational thought is born when the mythical mind begins distinctions and explanations.

Since myth is the primary form of consciousness, it exerts an influence over all the other symbolic forms, in Cassirer's view. Therefore, in order to understand reality further it is necessary to understand the phenomena of myth, its development in culture and its role as revealer of value and gateway to the sacred. Cassirer insists upon a unity which the human spirit is constantly seeking through all the symbolic forms. He is opposed to allegorical interpretations on the grounds that the latter reduces myth to some other mode of truth, such as philosophy, theology, or history. This reductionism does not take into account the unique and irreducible element in mythical expression.

Cassirer demonstrates how language frees itself from the mythical context and how the notion of language as a distinct symbolic form emerges. Languages then give rise to metaphysics, to religion, and to science. Cassirer's explanation parallels the following conclusions of Bernard Lonergan in which he describes the process from mythic consciousness and its images through rational distinction and critical explanation to the explanation framed in metaphor and images.

> (1) that the world of pure science and of metaphysics is somehow very different from the world of poetry and of common sense,
>
> (2) that the apprehension of explanation stands in opposition and tension with the flow of sensitive presentations, of the feelings and emotions, of the talking and doing that form the palpable part of our living with persons and our dealing with things,
>
> (3) that as explanation is reached through description, so it must be applied concretely by turning from explanation back to the descriptive world of things for us, and therefore
>
> (4) that man's explanatory self-knowledge can become effective in his concrete living only if the content of systematic insights, the direction of judgments, the dynamism of decisions can be embodied in images that release feeling and emotion and flow spontaneously into deeds no less than words.[18]

Lonergan also makes the point that mythic consciousness is the absence of a critical type of self-knowledge and that myth is a consequence of mythic consciousness as metaphysics is a corollary to critical self-knowledge.[19] Myth and metaphysics are opposites; as metaphysics advances and withdraws from myth it develops its own language and terms for its explanation of reality. For Lonergan, however, the dialectic of the mind operates according to the triad myth-metaphysics-mystery. Mysteries ''are the dynamic images which make sensible to human sensitivity what human intelligence reaches for or grasps.''[20] These mysteries bring us back to the concept of myth which also grasps through symbol and image what human intelligence reaches for, but now the myth is conscious of itself as imagery which reveals and veils the mystery of being. Mystery, however, since it is related to myth, reverts into myth and the dialectic commences again. Each movement of the dialectic, however, results in a greater self-consciousness and a greater contraction of the known-unknown: "For just as it is true that nearly all we say is metaphor, so also it is true that metaphor is revised and contracted myth and that myth is anticipated and expanded metaphor."[21] The allegorical aspect of myth appears when myth is conceived as a solution to a problem of expression. It is at this point that myth is the language of literature, the language of the self.

Northrop Frye claims that myth is an important aspect of literary criticism because it is an integral element of literature.[22] In his discussion of myth, Frye states that both plot and narrative are a translation of Aristotle's *mythos* by which Aristotle meant plot and narrative or *lexis*.[23] While Lévi-Strauss claims that the translation of myth is the moment when the translator cannot be called "betrayer" or that translation is at its lowest betraying value, Frye claims that any rendering of myth in more conceptual language does not give the real equivalent of the myth: "No rendering of myth into conceptual language can serve as a full equivalent of its meaning. A myth may be told and retold: it may be modified or elaborated, or different patterns may be discovered in it; and its life is always the poetic life of a story, not the homiletic life of some illustrated truism."[24] A verbal universe is the end of the mythical structure. This structural principle of mythology, which is the result of analogy and identity, in due course becomes the very structural principle of literature as well.[25] In literature Frye calls this indirect mythologizing, displacement: "by displacement I mean the techniques a writer uses to make his story credible, logically motivated or morally acceptable—lifelike, in short. I call it displacement for many reasons, but one is that fidelity to the credible is a feature of literature that can affect only content."[26]

Frye concludes his essay with a statement on the inextricable relationship of literature and myth: "With the literary category we reach a dead end, until we realize that literature is a reconstructed mythology, with its structural principles derived from those of myth."[27] Therefore, the mythology of literature is composed of a shape whose center is the order of words.

Frye's *Anatomy of Criticism* is an extensive study of myth. In his chapter entitled "Theory of Myths," he defines the relationship of myth to narration: "In terms of narrative, myth is the imitation of actions near or at the conceivable limits of desire."[28] Here he refines his first definition by claiming that mythical structure is present even in realistic fiction through "displacement." For him, myth stands at one pole of literary design and naturalism at the other, and in between is the area of romance.[29] The entire essay as well as the book *Anatomy of Criticism* offer very valuable insights into the relationship of mythology and literature.

In a study of English romanticism, Northrop Frye continues his treatment of the mythological world of literature. He claims here, too, that the informing structures of literatures are myths. His first chapter, "The Romantic Myth," is a valuable contribution to the history of myth in preromantic literature. In this essay he also develops the theme of identity and its relationship with myth. The myth of Creation, the Fall, and cyclical rebirth involve man in his loss of identity as well as the regaining of identity. In the preromantic mythology man's identity was not one founded upon a relationship with nature but on opposition to nature: "To regain his true identity man had to keep the barrier of consciousness against nature, and to think of himself first as a social being."[30] Poetry, however, unites man with nature by the most elementary forms of union and identification such as analogy, simile, and metaphor. Through romanticism's identification of man and nature, the subject-object tension is obliterated: "One's relationship to the rest of life then becomes a participating relationship, an identity of process rather than a separation of subjective and objective creatures or products."[31]

In romanticism the thrust for identity resulted in more earth-centered than "upward" metaphors. Heaven and hell and the older preromantic mythologies became the identity and alienation myths of the romantic mythologies. The search for man's identity is founded on his oneness and his participation in nature, not on his opposition to it. His lack of identity comes from his alienation from other people and nature rather than from his alienation from God. The essay is completed by Northrop Frye in these words: "To sum up: any given literature is rooted in a specific culture and is contained by the mythical structure of that culture."[32]

In conclusion, the different approaches to mythology, the anthropological, philosophical, and literary, all show the importance of myth in the experience of man. Myth is central to an understanding of who man is. The stories that he tells and the words that he uses define man's given culture and his mythology as they reciprocally define him. Since every mythology is made up of words, the words are the significant, informing sources of the myth. While Lévi-Strauss may claim that myth mediates among contradictions and is the most translatable of stories, the retelling of the myth and the recalling of the myth is a basically sacred, religious function. While the myth may relate something past, the *in illo tempore* of Eliade, its remembering recreates and brings into being something new. Hardly inferior to other ways of looking at reality, mythical consciousness, as Cassirer points out, creates language. Language is more the result of mythical consciousness than it is of discursive reasoning and later becomes the tool of this discursive reasoning. However, as Lonergan points out, metaphor and simile, the important tools of myth, become inescapable and inevitable for language particularly in translating metaphysics into a descriptive language, a communicable sign. Frye teaches that myth tells man where he stands, either as alienated from God in the heaven-hell stories, or alienated from himself and nature in the naturalistic narratives. The words of the myth, the structure of the myth, are all attempts at recovering identity. This search for the self, then, is inseparable from the necessity for words. Yet while words in their origin discriminate and differentiate, they also form images of *unity* which by nature they cannot embody.

## MYTH, WORD, AND SELF

### *The Unnamable*—Samuel Beckett

It is important to understand the relationship of myth to the structure of the novels of Samuel Beckett as well as of Proust, Joyce, Faulkner, Lawrence, Gide. In Samuel Beckett's *The Unnamable,* critics have found more philosophy at times than mythology and literature. In fact, Susan Sontag makes this statement about Beckett's critics: "Beckett's delicate dramas of the withdrawn consciousness—pared down to essentials, cut off, often represented as physically immobilized—are read as a statement about modern man's alienation from meaning or from God, or as an allegory of psychopathology."[33] She insists that "interpretation based on the highly dubious theory that a work of art is composed of items of content violates art."[34] The very valid point Susan Sontag makes concerning the inseparability of form and content suggests that a great work of art perfectly weds form to content and that to divorce them means violation. This does not mean, however, that the work of art does not seek to be understood. The importance of the reader's structuring ability in relationship to the form of the novel, especially the *nouveau roman*, will follow in a later chapter.

The form of *The Unnamable* seems to be chaos constantly on the verge of cosmos. The "I" of *The Unnamable* is an I who relates to many selves, an I in search of a name, a world. If one is to accept the naming of an object in the mythical sense as the calling into being of the object or the person and the lack of a name as the noncalling into being, *The Unnamable,* with an understanding of the fundamental meaning of the word mythical, is a novel concerned with the search for existence, for being, for definition. Frederick Hoffman, in *The Language of Self,* claims that all Beckett's novels deal with the self: "The basic materials of Beckett's work are selves as inquiring beings, selves as objects, other objects, and the degrees and forms of distance between one of these and another."[35]

From another aspect the novels can be seen as parodies of the creation myth. In the previous treatment of language and mythology it was observed that the word has creative power. In this context the I of *The Unnamable* realizes that his existence depends upon finding the right words which will call the I into being. He has spent so many of his words on others, either his creations or his creators: "All these Murphy's, Molloys and Malones do not fool me. They have made me waste my time, suffer for nothing, speak of them when, in order to stop speaking, I should have spoken of me and me alone."[36] The Unnamable is torn between speaking and not speaking. While he craves the silence, he also knows that once the silence begins he has ended his search for existence: "you must go on, I can't go on, you must go on, I'll go on, you must say words, as long as there are any, until they find me" (p. 414). Therefore, all words must be spoken since all are differentiated from, reflectors of, a single unnamable source.

Words are the solution, the creation, the creative material for the I. It is a terrible torment for the I not to know who he is, to want to stop speaking and yet to realize that unless he continues his parodies at creation, he cannot call himself into being. While silence is a torment for the Unnamable, words seem inadequate for his arrival at being: "it's the fault of the pronouns, there is no name for me, no pronoun for me, all the trouble comes from that, that, it's a kind of pronoun too, it isn't that either, I'm not that either" (p. 404). The Unnamable seems to be an "almost" word, alone in the beginning. He parodies all creations in his aloneness. He asks whether Basil, Mahood, and Worm are parts of him or are different from him, or whether they are names with which he confuses himself. In this tension between the names of the others who may have his own name, names of himself, his creations, or his creators, the Unnamable exclaims that he is none of these. Their names don't satisfy him:

Decidedly Basil is becoming important, I'll call him Mahood instead, I prefer that, I'm queer. It was he told me stories about me, lived in my stead, issued forth from me, came back to me, entered back into me, heaped stories on my head. I don't know how it was done. I always liked not knowing, but Mahood said it wasn't right . . . He didn't know either, but it worried him. It was his voice which has often, always, mingled with mine, and sometimes drowned it completely. (P. 309)

These people called Mahood and Basil, the Unnamable claimed, spoke to him, taught him lessons, left him, returned to him again; yet, they remained mysteries to him. The fact that he named them, however, means that he called them into existence, although he doubts their existence at times. "I shall not be alone in the beginning. I am of course alone. Alone" (p. 292). It doesn't really matter whether the Unnamable is alone or not. What does matter is that he does not know who he is and in his attempt to find out who he is he needs words, he needs language, he needs to find a name so that other existences and previous personae can witness his existence. The need for words has an ambivalent attraction in this respect. While they give a name, a definition, and an existence, they also have a way of becoming an obstacle in the path to the self. In this role they become a most pervasive type of witness, perpetrating distinction, multiplying personae, and fixing the person in immobile categories. This is the reason the Unnamable can say he likes the silence before the words.

Actually, it is only the words and language which witness his existence, but none of them are able to give him the definition and identity he needs. While the Unnamable says that he is suffering, he tells his story humorously. He claims that tears are rolling down his face and that is how he knows that he is, that his suffering rather than his thought is his proof of existence and that his name was forgotten by him. He asks himself about Basil, whether it was he who stole his name and took his existence away from him, but receives no answer: "Is he still usurping my name, the one they foisted on me, up there in their world, patiently, from season to season?" (p. 298).

The oscillation between creating and being created, between having a name and no name, between silence and words, between nonbeing and identity, form the structure of the novel. The fact that the novel does not have a plot is not important. Its narrative form, its blocks of words, parodies the creation of a self. The style of *The Unnamable* is markedly a humorous one. The tone, in spite of the anxious quest of the narrator, becomes parodic.

In most of the definitions, mythical structure has been characterized by a drive toward the reconciliation of opposites. If the syntax of *The Unnamable* is analyzed from this point of view, the structure that comes to light is primitively mythical in its repetition of polarities struggling for mediation. A typical instance is the insistence with which the Unnamable continues: "I can't go on, I'll go on, you must go on, I'll go on" (p. 414). These contradictions are examples in which the myth seeks some kind of unity. It is through this repetitive contradiction that the structure of the novel takes shape. Since myth, too, is concerned with the origin of things, the Unnamable is concerned with his origin. He wants to recall the stories that he told. Perhaps Murphy, Watt, Molloy, or Malone, his fictions which his word called into existence, could explain him. Yet they seem of little help here, for it is the language of the Unnamable which describes and concretizes the I's search for a self. It is the word, the name, which calls the self into being and separates it from Murphy, Molloy, Malone, Basil, Mahood, and Worm. The Unnamable knows that he must ironically continue in this way to contradict himself, to repeat himself, until he finds the adequate yet imprisoning word which will forever capture his personal being.

The I of the Unnamable sounds at times like the persona of Samuel Beckett, particularly when the I alludes to the other novels of Beckett. With the I as a possible persona, the emphasis on the creator giving himself a name, distinguishing himself from his characters as well as identifying himself with them, becomes very pronounced. While the I of the Unnamable seems to be at times the mask of Beckett, the other characters of the novel are projections and personae of the I whom he accepts and describes. In his attempt to find the real self, the I realizes that he is at the same time all of these characters and none of them. The ironic, humorous and transformed shapes of these people give the search for the self symbolic meaning. This means that all these deformed shapes and characters are not the I, otherwise he would know who he is; rather, they are fictions and names of the I. They are masks and, consequently, creations, or perhaps, creators and namers of the I.

The tension between creation and creator, being alone and with another, silence and words, are all part of the fabric of the mythical structure of *The Unnamable*. In the style of this novel and the continual flow of contradictions and humor, the reality of the creation emerges and becomes the fiction of order and the chief characteristic of the I. In Eliade's terminology the progression from chaos to cosmos is the mythical pattern. Just as this novel is far from a metaphysical treatise, it is also far from a novel in which content is grounded in rational explanation. The reader must almost be hypnotized by the words, by the contradictions, and by the tensions of polarities. He must read the book aloud sometimes to hear for himself a story that seems to be told *in illo tempore*:

> you must go on, that's all I know, they're going to stop me, I know that well, I can feel it, they're going to abandon me, it will be the silence, for a moment, a good few moments, or it will be mine, the lasting one, that didn't last, that still lasts, it will be I, you must go on, I can't go on, you must go on, I'll go on, you must say words, as long as there are any, until they find me, until they say me, strange pain, strange sin, you must go on, perhaps it's done already, perhaps they have said me already, perhaps they have carried me to the threshold of my story, before the door that opens on my story, that would surprise me, if it opens, it will be I, it will be the silence, where I am, I don't know, in the silence you don't know, you must go on, I can't go on, I'll go on. (P. 414)

The "they" as opposed to the "I" who carries the "me" to the threshold of his story, perhaps, is a "they" who could be the words, who are the Basils and the Mahoods and the Worms, the masks of the Unnamable. They are all those who through words would bring the not yet I into being. The multiplicity of contradictions, the driving force of the words, the constant flow, always produce the effect of a being who is not yet. The Unnamable, therefore, is not yet I or he or me. For, as he said, "if it opens, it will be I, it will be the silence where I am" (p. 414). Silence is identified with the individual world before its creation as well as the I. Words are seen both as an obstacle to the I and as the only way toward being. The Unnamable claims "I don't know, I'll never know, in the silence you don't know" (p. 414). His attempted words include, therefore, contradictions, the search for mediation, the repetition of the story and all the mythical energy needed to progress from chaos

51

to cosmos and allow the not yet I to have a name. They also continually seek the moment immediately preceding the story, the silence at the threshold. Once this name is had, the Unnamable also has a cosmos. The rhythm of the story is persistent, and its search is a process: "you must go on, I can't go on, you must go on, I'll go on" (p. 414). The person in *The Unnamable* is a nondefined person because he has not been named. He has words which function as the product of his mythical consciousness as well as the tools of rational discourse; they are the only aid he has in his pursuit. The "person" in *The Unnamable* is one on a quest, a never-ending quest toward being, toward definition. His reality is always a reality defined in a not yet state. He will continue, however, with the incantation: "I can't go on, I'll go on" (p. 414).

## MYTH, STORY, AND SELF

Paralleling the voice in *The Unnamable* who is hoping to be brought to the threshold of his story, the voices of William Faulkner are persistent in their search for existence. While the speaker in *The Unnamable* keeps repeating sentences, the voices of William Faulkner's *Absalom, Absalom!, The Sound and The Fury*, and *As I Lay Dying* repeat stories. The stories are repeated either by different narrators seeking to arrive at the truth or by a character who is the object of the stories such as Addie in *As I Lay Dying*. Since the narrative structures in *Absalom, Absalom!* and *As I Lay Dying* have a very clear relationship with both mythology and language, they will be explored in terms of the search for the self behind this mythical structure and linguistic narrative.

### *Absalom, Absalom!*

Before the discussion of the relationship between the story and the self in *Absalom, Absalom!,* a short description of the self and possessions may be helpful in seeing the significance of Sutpen's dream. One of the most prevalent subconscious means of identification for many Americans is by possession. The American dream, as satirized by writers like Nathanael West in *A Cool Million,* implies that money and possessions encourage a securer sense of identity. For example, Peter is Peter and not John because he has this particular house, these friends, vacations in such and such a place, has this kind of car, this type of job, and makes so much money. While some of this may be valid in terms of defining self, an emphasis on possessions which obscures other more human values makes identity the result of opposition to other people. This opposition can set up a system of alienation in which private property becomes the absolute and "others" become threats to this absolute. In the dynasty which Sutpen seeks to found in *Absalom, Absalom!*, for instance, there is implicit the obsession which self-definition in terms of possession may suggest. Identity seen in terms of possession can obliterate the human truths implicit in dialogue which is founded on the brotherhood of the human heart transcending color, nationality, and prosperity.

The tragedy and aspirations of Sutpen, however, are larger than the American dream. They are founded on something much more basic for man : his openness to infinity. To show both the magnitude of this dream as well as the smallness of it, Faulkner clothes the tales in a mythical structure which has overtones suggestive of many meanings.

Most critics see the relevance of the Absalom story to myth in the novel's title which echoes the words of David over his dead son, Absalom : "My son, Absalom! Absalom, my son, my son!"[37] David, like Sutpen, desired to found a dynasty in which his need for sons was a *sine qua non*. The mythological fabric which the title as well as the plot suggest makes up the indirect mythologizing which, in a realist structure, is called by Northrop Frye "displacement." The framework of the novel has to do with the identity of Sutpen, a modern David anxious to found a dynasty. The reality of Sutpen, however, is the reality which each of the storytellers, each of the narrators, gives him. In fact, as each narrator tries to reconstruct the story of Sutpen, he is, in fact, writing his own biography, is defining himself. Since the story defines the storyteller, the storyteller often seems as anxious to find out who he is as he is to find out the reality of the Sutpen story. His own reality is defined in relationship to Sutpen and in what he makes of the myth attached to the story. While the story always defines the storyteller, the characters' search for identity in the fabric of words admits of degrees of explicitness. For instance Shreve and Mr. Compson seem less explicitly interested in their own identity than Quentin or Miss Rosa.

In the narrative structure of *Absalom, Absalom!* the search for the real Sutpen takes place through the narrator's search and telling of his own story. Quentin seems to understand this about Miss Rosa as she tells him Sutpen's story apologetically. After she apologizes for taking up his afternoon, since she thought he wanted to be in another place, he answers : "Only she don't mean that, he thought . . . It's because she wants it told.''[38] The narration, or the telling of the story in its most primitive energy, is also the story of the narrator. The narrator must tell his story, re-create the character of Sutpen, for in doing so he is re-creating himself whether he be Shreve, Quentin, Miss Rosa Coldfield, or whoever. Faulkner suggests this relativity of point of view in his response to the question about narration in this novel:

> I think that no individual can look at truth. It blinds you. You look at it and you see one phase of it. But taken all together, the truth is in what they saw though nobody saw the truth intact. So these are true as far as Miss Rosa and as Quentin saw it. Quentin's father saw what he believed was truth, that was all he saw. But the old man was himself a little too big for people no greater in stature than Quentin and Miss Rosa and Mr. Compson to see all at once. It would have taken perhaps a wiser or more tolerant or more sensitive or more thoughtful person to see him as he was. It was, as you say, thirteen ways of looking at a blackbird. But the truth, I would like to think, comes out, that when the reader has read all these thirteen ways of looking at a blackbird, the reader has his own fourteenth image of that blackbird which I would like to think is the truth.[39]

The reader's fourteenth viewpoint is founded on the epistemological structure which determines his own identity and persona as well as his understanding of the Sutpen story. Early in the novel, Faulkner sets the narrative structure and consequently determines the reader's response in an atmosphere of creative energy. Miss Rosa, who regards Sutpen as a demon, tells her story as well as Sutpen's in a setting which echoes creation. Paralleling Sutpen's symbol of a god creating a dream in his dynasty ambition, Miss Rosa, the first narrator, also parodies the words of Yahweh: ''Let there be light.'' Faulkner reinforces this through the significant intrusion of his own voice reminding the reader that Quentin is listening and creating while Rosa Coldfield is constructing her version of the Sutpen cosmos:

> Then in the long unamaze Quentin seemed to watch them overrun suddenly the hundred square miles of tranquil and astonished earth and drag house and formal gardens violently out of the soundless Nothing and clap them down like cards upon a table beneath the up-palm immobile and pontific, creating the Sutpen's Hundred, the *Be Sutpen's Hundred* like the oldentime *Be Light*.[40]

This creation of Rosa also parallels the drive found in Quentin's need to reconstruct the story. As Quentin makes reasons for Rosa's story, he finds himself split in two. There is a tremendous contrast between the setting in which the novel begins and the way in which it ends. Both parts are narrated by the persona of the author and both show the two Quentins who are listening to the story: the first Quentin, who on a very hot September afternoon is finding re-created for him the story of Sutpen, and the second Quentin, who has already heard Rosa's version of the story and other versions as well but who must make up his own version and search through the retelling of the story for a meaning to his own life:

> Then hearing would reconcile and he would seem to listen to two separate Quentins now—the Quentin Compson preparing for Harvard in the South, the deep South dead since 1865 and peopled with garrulous outraged baffled ghosts, listening, having to listen, to one of the ghosts which had refused to lie still even longer than most had, telling him about ghost-times: and the Quentin Compson who was still too young to deserve to be a ghost, but nevertheless having to be one for all that, since he was born and bred in the deep South the same as she was—the two separate Quentins now talking to one another in the long silence of notpeople, in notlanguage. (P. 9)

The two Quentins are fused into one in spite of the fact that Quentin is so self-conscious that he sees himself seeing Rosa and hears himself listening to her as he makes up his own story about Sutpen, which is ultimately a story about himself and his "genesis."

The beginning of the novel is set in a context of stifling heat. Miss Coldfield and Quentin sit from two o'clock until almost sundown in a room that is "dim, hot and airless," with the blinds closed. The afternoon is described as "a hot, weary and dead September afternoon." The hot, dead, unmoving air is penetrated only by the heavy odor of flowers. This contrasts with the setting of the end of the novel. Here Quentin responds to Shreve's question about hating the South in "the cold air, the iron New England dark." Actually it is Quentin who is recalling in the cold New England dark the hot September afternoon in which he first heard the Sutpen story and remembers himself listening. In this dark the never ending re-creation of the story takes place. In retelling the myth Quentin is trying to understand himself better. The words of darkness and death have a meaning which is in stark contrast to the light which is suggested by the search for the true Sutpen. Into this dark atmosphere the words "Let there be light," the Word itself, comes in order to bring into existence, into the presence of the tellers, the being of Sutpen. While the narrators are giving their version of the story, each reader, moreover, is reconstructing and structuring his own story.

The truth about Sutpen must be discovered. Is he a demon, a Faustus, a Beelzebub, a god? Sutpen wonders about this himself. He is here, at least, a god or a demiurge:

> You see, I had a design in my mind. Whether it was a good or a bad design is beside the point; the question is, Where did I make the mistake in it, what did I do or misdo in it, whom or what injure by it to the extent which this would indicate. I had a design. To accomplish it I should require money, a house, a plantation, slaves, a family—incidentally of course, a wife. (P. 263)

The creator image is extended into a Trinitarian image by which Mr. Compson, Quentin, and Shreve become one. In Quentin's words: "Maybe we are both, Father. Maybe nothing ever happens once and is finished . . . Yes, we are both, Father. Or maybe Father and I are both Shreve, maybe it took Father and me both to make Shreve or Shreve and me both to make Father or maybe Thomas Sutpen to make all of us" (pp. 261–262). It is by this mutual self-definition which each telling of the story engenders that Thomas Sutpen is creating all other characters. The power of the "creator story" is linked with the narrator's quest to recapture the past. Sutpen, however, exists only in the words of the narrators. In terms of the Trinitarian structure, Thomas Sutpen, the father, has allowed his word to be for the reader the visible sign of his presence. In this way the very close relationship between the father and the word, his sign, form a bond relating the Trinitarian structure and the creation story.

The direct mythical material which Faulkner uses certainly finds its clue in the title, *Absalom, Absalom!* This material with its reference to the Old Testament story of David and Absalom shapes the more explicit displacement elements in the novel. Like Sutpen, David has a first son, Amnon, whom he does not recognize as being the fit continuer of his kingdom. Amnon, moreover, falls in love with his half-sister and finally rapes her. Both David and his son Absalom are angry with him for this. David, however, does not want to harm Amnon because he loves him.

Absalom, on the other hand, kills him because of the incest. The news of this torments David. He is only reassured by the words of his brother: "Let not my Lord the King imagine that all the King's sons are dead; Amnon alone is dead and Absalom has taken flight."[41] Immediately before Amnon's death David had lost another son because of his own sin with Uriah's wife. As with Sutpen, David's kingdom is destroyed by his own sins. The sons that they want so badly are doomed because of the failings of the father. Finally Absalom, Henry's parallel, is killed. The words of Absalom before his death reinforce the failure of the dynasty: " 'I have no son,' he said 'to preserve the memory of my name!' " (2 Sam. 18:18). Consequently, David's adultery, his son's fratricide, and his son's and daughter's incest are all parts of the more explicit mythical structure which Faulkner uses in the novel. These references complement the less direct myth-making found in the "creator" and "Trinitarian" images.

Faulkner said at the University of Virginia (1957–1958) that Sutpen was a tragedy of a man who wanted sons, who wanted too many and that they eventually destroyed him. It is into this fabric of story telling that Faulkner weaves fragments of Hebrew myth such as the creation account, the Absalom story, and the Christian explanation of God and its Trinitarian dimensions.

There are also displaced fragments of Greek myth present in the novel. In his innocence, Sutpen becomes like the blind Oedipus who is not able to recognize that the evil and suffering in his kingdom are traceable to himself. He and his sons are also echoes of Orestes, pursued by the Eumenides because of domestic sin. In the design of the dynasty and in the domestic crises of adultery, fratricide, incest, and blind guilt, the primitive energy of the Hebrew and Greek stories merge. Through this structuring, Faulkner projects the tale of Sutpen beyond any one man or self and gives it universal significance. The form of the novel confirms the universality of the story: of Quentin's search, of Sutpen's, of Rosa's search, and so on. In this context, it is ironic for the reader to remember, as he hears about Jim Bond from Shreve at the end of the novel, that the title refers to the failure of a dream which transcends time. The novel forces the reader constantly to oscillate from the son to the father, from the dreamed to the dreamer, from the created to the creator, from the narrated to the narrators. In this context Sutpen himself becomes both the created and the creator, and it is very significant that Quentin understands Thomas Sutpen as making all the characters.

Since much of the exploration in the novel centers around the fate of Sutpen's design, Rosa claims that he was a demon and his plan was doomed to failure. Mr. Compson, however, claims that it was Sutpen's innocence which destroyed his plan. He believes that Sutpen did what he did not because he wanted to do it, but because he needed to do it so that he could live with himself and be himself. Mr. Compson expresses Sutpen's innocence in moral categories. His particular perspective views Sutpen's innocence or lack of it as the real key to his tragedy: "that innocence which believed that the ingredients of morality were like the ingredients of pie or cake and once you had measured them and balanced them and mixed them and put them into the oven it was all finished and nothing but pie or cake could come out" (p. 263). This oven type of morality becomes the Sutpen Hundred burning to the ground with the howling idiot running out. The outcome may seem to be Faulkner's agreement with Mr. Compson's judgment on Sutpen. On the other hand, Faulkner would not favor Mr. Coldfield's point of view, or rather, Rosa's understanding of Mr. Coldfield's statement that the edifice failed because it was founded "not on the rock of stern morality but on the shifting sands of opportunism and moral brigandage" (p. 260). Coldfield's puritanism is as much based on hypocritical values of abstractions and escapism as Sutpen's is based on external respectability. While Faulkner suggests that none of his narrators is completely reliable, his own voice seems to come through at times. Faulkner's presence pervades the underlying myth of the novel and makes itself clearly felt in the "they" of the opening sentence as Faulkner introduces the setting where Rosa Coldfield and Quentin Compson are conversing.

In all of this the name, word, and story are important for identity, for being: "He named her himself. He named them all himself" (p. 61). The naming that Sutpen does as creator and the words that each of the narrators use during their re-creation of Sutpen are really manifestations of what they do not yet know. In telling the story they are learning about Sutpen, making Sutpen up as well as learning about themselves. It is here that the story and language ascend in importance. Both before the story is told and afterward, Sutpen is incomplete. For in the telling of the story, Sutpen's identity is determined by the incomplete perspective of each storyteller. The words become tools for understanding, and, unless the word is spoken, there is nothing to be understood. One word leads to another and yet another until there is a story, until that story is retold by another narrator and yet another until all become creatures of their own creation. The narration, then, compels both narrators and readers to the center where Sutpen seems to reside. Yet Sutpen's real self is as elusive as the center of an onion. The reality of Sutpen must be searched for through the maze of the narrator's and reader's constructions.

The words are the tools of the story and form labyrinths of understanding, but the mirror images in the novel are also important. The son, himself the word and mirror of the father, mirrors the father in the word; this expands the Trinitarian image in the novel. (The early Christian fathers spoke of the Son as not only the Word of the Father, but as his mirror, also.) One of the most obvious mirror images is that of Charles Bon, the son, and Thomas Sutpen, the father. Charles Bon is a testament to the humanity which Thomas flees. Charles, like Thomas, has a Negro wife whom he rejects for more calculated but yet for less than human reasons. Both Charles and the father he reflects seem unforgivable violators of the human heart; yet, like his father, the fact of his humanity haunted Charles and gnawed at him, thus eliciting sympathy in the reader. Henry, too, is the accepted son of the father (the Absalom of the story), and his father's mirror. While Thomas is a man of thought (for his plan involves a great projection), Thomas and Mr. Compson view Henry as a man who feels and acts immediately and who never thinks (p. 96).

The farther away the Sutpens withdrew from their humanity the more the mirror image became distorted and parodied. This is particularly true in the relationship of Thomas Sutpen and Jim Bond, the idiot grandson of Charles. Perhaps this is the final comment on Sutpen's design : the ultimate idiocy of a great plan. Even more suggestive is the line in the geneology about Jim: "whereabouts unknown" (p. 383). The real Sutpen perhaps, like Jim Bond, is unknown; he is not unknowable, however, because each reader creates his own Sutpen and his own Jim Bond. Recognizing that he never really gets an objective account from the fragments of narrative structure, each reader must make his own decision, he must make his own story with the varied tools and creations of the narrators and of the principal storyteller who frames the novel in its mythical dimensions and entitles it *Absalom, Absalom!* Sutpen exists only in the space between the narrator and the reader. He exists in the overreaching of every man's ambition.

Sutpen's story is as old as man and is as mysterious and tragic as his many dreams. The real Sutpen lies beyond the narrator, the reader, and even Faulkner, and finds himself in the inherited, mysterious energy of man's lack of knowledge of himself and of the consequences of his designs. Joyce said it well in his articulation of the son's ever constant striving for atonement with the father. The son in this context is both creator and created. He is at the same time the creature and word of the storytellers and the creator of his own dream. Both aspects of this reality are reconciled through the structuring ability of man as he seeks to define himself in his relationship to others. The whole pattern of the novel suggests the father's need to find his meaning in a son and the need of a creator to understand himself in creatures of his making. The quest of Sutpen is as much the dynastic father's quest toward self as it is the result of each storyteller's and each reader's desire to know the real Sutpen; with Sutpen and his narrators the reader in his search seems to walk toward an infinitely receding horizon of identity.

## As I Lay Dying

The problem of words betraying the self as well as creating it is explicitly stated by Addie of *As I Lay Dying*. In technique and form, however, this novel is very different from *Absalom, Absalom!* and more closely resembles *The Sound and the Fury*. In structure, however, *As I Lay Dying* is somewhat more elaborate than *The Sound and the Fury*, since it involves many more differentiated points of view. Instead of four large sections, there are many short chapters in which fifteen characters describe some part of Addie's funeral procession. Each of these descriptions defines the character or the personality of the observer. The search for self, in this case, is seen from an almost omniscient point of view by the reader; he hears one character after another express his views on Addie, on her death, and on life itself.

As Sutpen is the center of *Absalom, Absalom!*, Addie is the center of *As I Lay Dying*. It is she who motivates the funeral procession to Jefferson. The Bundrens' goal is to find themselves, and somehow their relationship to Addie is the key to their identity. They must explore themselves in terms of Addie.

Olga Vickery sees the whole journey to Jefferson as a travesty of the ritual of interment: "Because the agonizing journey to Jefferson does fulfill the promise to Addie, because it does reunite her in death with her family, some critics have seen in it an inspiring gesture of humanity or a heroic act of traditional morality. In reality, however, the journey from beginning to end is a travesty of the ritual of interment."[42] Some critics have given this a religious interpretation, particularly because of Addie's words to Cora in which she speaks of her son, Jewel, the result of her sin, as her cross and her salvation. ''He is my cross and he will be my salvation. He will save me from the water and from the fire. Even though I have laid down my life, he will save me.''[43]

Salvation through water and fire has many religious associations; it is especially resonant of the Old Testament pilgrimages through flood and fire. Faulkner uses these symbols very carefully in this setting, for they have an ironic significance. The Bundrens' serious commitment to the completion of the journey is deflated by the irony of the conclusion. Almost a parody of a parody, the journey is certainly ironic.

The ultimate consequences of the journey for each one of the Bundrens is different; to each Bundren, Jefferson means something different. For Darl, since he had gone completely mad, it means a train ride to Jackson. For Anse it means a new Mrs. Bundren, whom he marries for a Graphophone. For Dewey it means an abortion. The new false teeth, the new wife, and the bananas that Darl and Vardaman are eating as they view Anse's return with his new wife, all contribute to a very ironic ending for this serious funeral procession through fire and water and ultimately suggest that even the most serious plans of man are often undercut by his own inability to see his real motives. Some critics would like to see in the humorous end of the journey a statement that, ultimately, life itself is a joke.

There are, moreover, further religious and, in this sense, perhaps mythical dimensions to the story. Each character interprets the family events according to his experiences. For Vardaman, who does not know how to deal with the death of his mother and knows of death only from his experiences with a dead fish, his mother becomes a fish:

> My mother is a fish. Darl says that when we come to the water again I might see her and Dewey Dell said, She's in the box: how could she have got out? She got out through the holes I bored, into the water I said, and when we come to the water again I am going to see her. My mother is not in the box. My mother does not smell like that. My mother is a fish. (P. 483)

The symbolism of the fish is a means for Vardaman to cope with the reality of his mother's death. The fish is mentioned again when Dewey Dell remembers Vardaman sticking a knife into a fish. The interrelationship of symbols is very significant here, for water, fire, and fish all have mythical and religious overtones. These images recur and merge in the novel.

Even Addie's coffin resembles a fish. Since the early Christian sign of Christ was a fish, the meaning of Addie and her centrality to the understanding of the life of each of the characters is made even more blurred. Addie's crucifixion or death, her function as the savior as well as the saved, form part of the mystery in this narration. While Vardaman has to identify his mother with the fish to understand the phenomenon of her death, the fish symbol emerges in this context as another sign of the ambiguity of the procession. For the fish, the *ichthys,* is ultimately a soteriological sign, a salvific sign, and somehow Addie's burial is salvific. This salvation means a recovery of aspects of self which is always incomplete. During the final burial of the fish symbol at the end of the story, the humor is soteriological as well as parodic and presents the plight of the family in a sympathetic as well as a ludicrous light.

The fish, for Vardaman, is also an example of how association relates to self-identification. Vardaman knows who he is because Cash is his brother. Jewel's mother is a horse because Vardaman associates the horse with Jewel. Vardaman's mother is a fish because he has associated himself with the fish, something he once possessed. For Vardaman the problem of identity is fundamental; it results from relationships to people and things. Vardaman's human need for finding himself in relationship to his dead mother enables the symbol of the fish and its interment to unify the entire purpose of the procession. The unity occurs through the religious significance of both the fish and the procession. As Cora retells Addie's understanding of it, the fish as well as the procession means "salvation."

Basically the novel confronts the problem of the relationship between the experience and the word. In addition, the conflict between the word and the deed is certainly linked with the problem of identity. After Addie marries Anse she feels duty-bound to him, since the word love has no significance in her understanding of the relationship. She is obliged to him and expresses this emotional hollowness in the tension between the word love and the reality of the experience. Merely performing her duty, she gives Anse children. The link between fidelity to the word and identity is remarkably clarified: "I would be I; I would let him be the shape and echo of his word" (pp. 465–466). In this context the person actually equals the word. For instance, when Addie is thinking about Anse, she claims that he has a word for how he feels toward her: he says it is love. She, however, can not accept his word as having any meaning: "But then I realized that I had been tricked by words older than Anse or love, and that the same word had tricked Anse too, and that my revenge would be that he would never know I was taking revenge'' (p. 464).

The revenge, she goes on to explain, is her request to be buried in Jefferson. However, her story is permeated with the fact that her father had told her that being alive was getting ready to stay dead. She realizes that death for her is simply a word because Anse, although living, is dead to her, dead to her feelings. It is interesting to juxtapose the emptiness between Addie and Anse with the word—love—that marked the relationship. While Addie looks upon Anse as dead, Addie is physically dead in the novel. She is, however, ironically alive through her promise. Through the promise or the word that was bound up with her, she continues to be present.

While the person equals the word, it really doesn't make any difference what name the person has: ''It doesn't matter what they call them'' (p. 465). She realizes that the word is vacuous and not really terribly significant, that names are dupes because they don't really match reality. In fact, when Addie thinks about her shape, she leaves the nouns out; there is a blank in the page. ''I would think: the shape of my body where I used to be a virgin is in the shape of a ———.'' Since words connote persons and since persons are merely the echoes of words, the words themselves are betrayers: they are merely fleeting shadows of what the experience is. As she lay down by Anse she used to hear all of this:

> I would lie by him in the dark . . . hearing the dark voicelessness in which the words are the deeds, and the other words that are not deeds, that are just the gaps in people's lacks coming down like the cries of the geese out of the wild darkness in the old terrible nights, fumbling at the deeds like orphans to whom are pointed out in a crowd the faces and told, that is your father and your mother. (P. 469)

It seems that Addie's search is for the word that matches the experience. She believes that she had found it in Whitfield, but his rhetoric is just as empty as her husband's. His confession to God is with empty words devoid of real feeling. He even rationalizes to himself that he is confessing to Anse although Anse is not there: ''But he is merciful. He will accept the will for the deed, who knew that when I framed the words of my confession it was to Anse I spoke them, even though he was not there''

(p. 469). The manner in which a person can be duped by words is part of the frame of reference of Addie's monologue.

Ironically, however, she, too, uses words in the interment promise to dupe and to betray as well. Addie, however, realizes this and is very self-conscious in her search for the link between the word and the deed, the word and the experience. She castigates Cora because words to Cora are empty: ''She prayed for me because she believed I was blind to sin, wanted me to kneel and pray too, because people to whom sin is just a matter of words, to them salvation is just words too'' (p. 468). For Cora and for Whitfield, salvation is just a matter of words. Whitfield makes his confession in words to God without any kind of real experience of regret. Cora just uses empty rhetoric as she tries to understand Addie. She can not understand how Addie ''sacrilegiously'' calls Jewel her cross and salvation in place of God. Addie's understanding of salvation is beyond that of words. For she knows that betrayal as well as fidelity is possible through words. She believes in Jewel, however. And Jewel, committed to action, saves her from the fire and the water in the journey and helps her corpse reach its destination, Jefferson.

The irony, however, is beyond Addie's promise because as soon as Addie dies Anse says, ''God's will be done, now I can get them teeth'' (p. 375). Anse's attitude toward words is one in which they are simply said like the names which were given their children. The meaning of words and identity are seen in Darl's insane ruminations: ''I don't know what I am. I don't know if I am or not.'' As he hears the rain falling and is trying to fall asleep, he realizes that to empty himself means that he is. The tautology of language emerges in this section as Darl tries to fall asleep. ''And since sleep is is-not and rain and wind are was, it is not'' (p. 396). The words of Darl can make anything be or not be depending on whether they are spoken. He can even be simply because he knows that he can say he is: ''And then I must be, or I could not empty myself for sleep in a strange room. And so if I am not emptied yet, I am is'' (p. 396).

The problem of identity, the idea of the I am, is a problem of the creative force of the spoken word. As Eliade claims, the word calls forth the presence of what it names; Addie would note that it doesn't infallibly produce the experience. Addie realizes how words can dupe man into thinking that there is a corresponding experience; yet there is not always one. Olga Vickery in her response to Addie claims that words can be adequate: ''Words need not, however, be empty providing they are grounded in non-verbal experience. It is when this condition is not met that they tend to be separated from and ultimately to replace the act.''[44]

Consequently, only when the word and the deed are united can the person become whole. Faithful to the experience of what she feels, Addie can give herself and be herself with Anse through duty, since this is what she feels and not love. It is only after realizing this that she can say: ''I would be I: I would let him be the shape and echo of his word.''[45] Both the word and the act must correspond before meaning can emerge, before the I can equal the I. When Addie has her relationship with Whitfield, she can say in this too that the word and the experience match. She can say it ''because he was he and I was I'' (p. 466). Addie repeats her father's adage that the reason for living is getting ready to stay dead and believes it because, when no more valid experiences correspond to the words, the person really is dead as Anse is in her mind. The promise, made to Addie by her family, in which word and experience coincide keeps her alive. Consequently, she is dying through the whole novel and never really dies until Anse comes out with the new Mrs. Bundren and his new false teeth. The whole family is now liberated to be their less than heroic selves.

## MYTH, DREAM, AND SELF

### *Finnegans Wake*—James Joyce

While it is true that one of the most intense searches for self may take place in conscious and waking life, there is also present in the subconscious activity of man the hidden search for self. In this respect, *Finnegans Wake* exemplifies how the language of the dream relates to the identity of a person. The dream provides an example of modern man's fragmentation as well as his subconscious attempts at integration. In a dream a much more free kind of search takes place while transpositions of names, of words, and consequently of persons mark the route. *Finnegans Wake,* at once Joyce's dream and the dream of Earwicker, produces a kind of mythical and archetypal search for self which the language of the novel mirrors. Since the novel has such a cosmic scope, it is difficult to treat *Finnegans Wake* in a chapter, and indeed a chapter could be spent on three or four sentences of the novel. Yet, treating the novel as a whole, from the standpoint of language transformation and personality transformation, provides a valuable insight into the nature of selfhood. For while Earwicker is searching and dreaming about himself, his search and his dreams become in Joyce's story the dream of man.

Language is very important here and its expression is not that of conscious rhetoric. In dream language, because of man's difficulty in confronting certain issues or problems, transformations of persons as well as of language occur. The contents of the dream may be more symbolic and seem even more elusive than rational language, nevertheless, there are overtones of meaning and possibilities of insights which are rich in significance.

The logic of *Finnegans Wake* is different from ordinary logic and must be accepted as different. For there is a logic to the irrationality of the dream and to the meaning of words that can only be discovered through conscious and critical research. Since a dream is not limited to time and space, Earwicker's dream transcends an historical moment and fuses past and present events. At once Earwicker can be God, Adam, Tristram, and Joyce. His sons can be part of himself, St. Michael the Archangel, the Devil. His daughter can be both Isabel and Iseult. His wife can be Eve as well as Anna. Time is seen *tota simul* in a dream. Because of this, the language found in a psychological experience which transcends time and space rings with the overtones of many languages. The fusion of syllables of many languages produces an experience which matches the creation of the word. The language transformations are particularly valuable in their significance, paralleling personality metamorphoses and changes. In this chapter, through the example of *Finnegans Wake*, the parallel between dream language and the self, or the relationship between the word of the dream and the name of the person is explored to add another dimension to the hidden self.

In Finnegans' dream the most perfect symbol of the fusion of time events from different ages and places is found in Vico's circular philosophy of history. Giovanni Baptista Vico (1668–1744) describes history in terms of a wheel. The events of history take place on a wheel, which means that the same events occur again and again. This is the significance of the end of the novel running into the first paragraph of the novel:

> A way a lone a last a loved a long the . . .
> River run, past Eve and Adam's, from swerve of shore to bend of bay, brings us by a commodius vicus of recirculation back to Howth Castle and Environs.[46]

This cyclical view of history is realized in the novel by the surfacing again and again of different transformations in names as well as in the persons about whom Earwicker or Joyce is dreaming.

One of the most frequently reoccurring changes is found in the names of the sons of Earwicker, Kevin and Jerry. They are not named explicitly until the end of the novel:

> And listening. So gladdied up when nicechild Kevin Mary (who was going to be commandeering chief of the choirboys' brigade the moment he grew up under all the auspices) irishsmiled in his milky way of cream dwibble and onage tustard and dessed tabbage, frighted out when badbrat Jerry Godolphing (who was hurrying to be cardinal scullion in a night refuge as bald as he was cured enough unerr all the hospitals) furrinfrowned down his winkly waste of methylated spirits, ick, and lemoncholy lees, ick, and pulverised rhubarbarorum, icky.
> Night by silentsailing night while infantina Isobel. (P. 555)

In this excerpt Earwicker's three children are named Kevin, Jerry, and Isobel. Throughout the novel all of their names and personalities undergo transformations. Different aspects of them are revealed. They become identified with different personages of history, forcing Earwicker himself to be identified with different heroes and personages. In the beginning of the novel, the reader is introduced to what eventually become Jerry and Kevin in the names Jhem and Shen. As his two sons become part of a historical event which happened in 1132 A. D. they are Caddy and Primas (p. 14). Most frequently, however, they are Shem and Shaun. Significant masks in the novel for Earwicker as well as for James Joyce, Shem and Shaun are aspects and personae of James Joyce while they are, in addition, complementary aspects of the personality of Earwicker who is the dream of an ultimate or chief persona of Joyce in the novel. While Earwicker is dreaming *"Semus sumus"* Joyce is too. Joyce, Earwicker's author, has Earwicker's dream that he is his son, Shem: "Shem is as short for Shemus as Jem is joky for Jacob" (p. 169).

Besides the obvious translation of "semus sumus," "we are Sem," there are more subtle identifications of Shem with Joyce. Shem is the author of the blue book of Eccles (which is *Ulysses*) since Bloom lives on 7 Eccles Street and is dreamed of as being criticized for his erotic language:

This explains the litany of septuncial lettertrumpets honorific, highpitched, erudite, neoclassical, which he so loved as partricianly to manuscribe after his name. It would have diverted, if ever seen, the shuddersome spectacle of this semidemented zany amid the inspissated grime of his glaucous den making believe to read his usylessly unreadable Blue Book of Eccles, *édition de ténèbres*, (even yet sighs the Most Different, Dr. Poindejenk, authorised bowdler and censor, it can't be repeated!) turning over three sheets at a wind, telling himself delightedly, no espellor mor so, that every splurge on the vellum he blundered over was an aisling vision more gorgeous than the one before t.i.t.s. (P. 179)

Earwicker is dreaming of the criticisms that Joyce had leveled against him for his composition of *Ulysses*. Here, Shem, the penman, is responsible for the novel. Shem, the son of Earwicker, becomes Earwicker himself as well as Joyce.

Guilt plays a great part in the reason for the transformation of names and persons. In fact, guilt emerges through two sources, sexual and theological. The theological source of guilt is clear in Joyce's relationship to the Church. Since Joyce was excommunicated for *Ulysses*, Shem, his persona, the son of Earwicker, is excommunicated:

John is a different butcher's. Next place you are up town pay him a visit. Or better still, come to buy. You will enjoy cattlemen's spring meat. Johns is now quite divorced from baking. Fattens, kells, flays, hangs, draws, quarters and pieces. Feel his lambs! Ex! Fell how sheap! Exex! His liver too is great value, a spatiality! Exexex! COMMUNICATED. (P. 172)

Shem also receives the criticisms that Joyce received. He composed this book for "luvvomony." He is an "antinomian." "The various meanings of all the different foreign parts of speech he misused" (p. 173). In other words, Shem was a guilty man; his artistry brought him a condemnation by the public, by Church leaders, and by literary critics.

In fact, Shem is Earwicker's way of facing that part in himself which is hard to accept and which at the same time is his genius. Earwicker is his son Shem and they are both personae for Joyce. Shem is guilty and he needs the purgation of the river. He is theologically guilty. "He is a fool, anarch, egoarch, hiresiarch." He needs the purgation of the river to clean him of his sin: "Let me see. It is looking pretty black against you, we suggest, Sheem avick. You will need all the elements in the river to clean you over it all and a fortifine popespriestpower bull of attender to booth'' (p. 188). Here the identification between Shem and Earwicker is very much fused. Throughout the novel Earwicker's wife, Anna Livia Plurabel, is symbolized by the river, while Earwicker is the mound or the hill. The river is necessary both as purgation and as life for Earwicker. Here the purgation of the river is needed for Shem, his son, as well as for his alter-ego. In his depths, Shem is guilty of lying through language because his accusers made him feel so guilty. Shem needs a brother, a complement, another aspect.

While critics have observed the identification of Shem with Joyce, they have overlooked the fact that Shaun embodies Joyce, too, since Shaun has been characterized by a moral arrogance. He is an aspect of Earwicker's personality as well as of Joyce's. This becomes clear particularly as the novel progresses. Shaun in Part III of the novel, carries a letter concerning Shem, his brother. He speaks about his brother, again in critical language. Not only is his brother theologically and linguistically guilty but also guilty sexually: ''I will describe you in a word. Thou. (I beg your pardon.) Homo! Then putting his bedfellow on me! (like into mike and nick onto post.)'' (p. 422). The feelings of guilt arising through the fear of homosexuality and incest in Earwicker are also reasons for the transformation in names. The element of guilt surrounding Shem's inadequacy and incompleteness is found in what Shaun says of him: ''As often as I think of that unbloody housewarmer, Shem Skrivenitch, always cutting my prhose to please his phrase, bogorror, I declare I get the jawache! Be me punting his reflection he'd begin his beogrefright in muddyass ribalds. Digteter! Grundtsagar! Swop beef!'' (p. 423).

Shaun not only echoes the language of literary critics but also of theological critics. Again, fragments of the excommunication: ''Ex. Ex. Ex. Ex.'' Shaun is requested by the listeners to tell of his brother, Shem, and he does in the story of the Grace Hoper and the Ondt (pp. 418–419). He is also asked and addressed by his listeners as ''kind Shawn'' (p. 421), ''Shaun Illustrious'' (p. 422), ''Thrice truthful teller, Shaun of grace?'' (p. 424). He is moreover identified with the teller of the tale as Sem was. ''*Semus sumus*'' finds its echo later in the novel in ''Jaunty Jaun, as I was shortly before that made aware'' (p. 429). Shaun becomes ''Juan,'' both a persona for Earwicker as well as brother to Shem and son of Earwicker. In this chapter, as well as in the preceding, Shaun is identified with light as Shem is identified with the darkness. Shaun, too, or Jaun, is an aspect of Earwicker and of Joyce. Juan, in this context, becomes a priest whose hands are cursed; he becomes a sermonizer, telling his sister what books to read and what books to avoid. He will seek to guard her and her virtue. Here Shaun, or Jaun, becomes identified with St. Michael the Archangel, as his brother, Shem is identified with the devil for his excommunication and his prose. Since he, Shaun, is identified with the Archangel Michael, who defends the church, Issy, Isabel, Iseult, the sister of Shaun becomes the Church.

Shaun or Juan is also changed to "Haun" (p. 472). While Shem is identified with the darker principle, the guilt, as well as the artist, and Shaun is identified with the light, the Defender, St. Michael, the moral conscience of the dream, Shaun, too, is an aspect of the dreamer. Shaun is a kind of conscience, the accusing as well as the defending conscience of Earwicker and of Joyce. Shaun is as incomplete a principle and as incomplete a person as Shem was. Shem and Shaun, brothers, sons of Earwicker, personae for him and Joyce, are also nonpersons. They are principles, or drives, which metamorphose into persons. Shem is the irrational as well as the artistic. Shaun is the rational, the limiter, the limiting, the conscience principle. Shaun is without guilt; Shem is accused by Shaun of guilt and of evil as the spokesman for society as well as for himself. Both these aspects or drives become masks for Earwicker; they are easier to face in different flesh than as aspects of himself. In Freudian terms, Shem represents that part of man which is responsible for creation, for the artistic as well as for the diabolic; Shaun represents the superego, conscience, and limiting principle. Both are incomplete and they call for a confrontation with Earwicker, but they can only be confronted in a dream.

The guilt which Shem is made to feel is an important aspect in the novel as it is in all dreams. Earwicker, who feels as if he is accused of something in Phoenix Park has his own feelings of guilt translated into other terms. The incident in Phoenix Park, first of all, may never have really occurred. For Earwicker, however, it becomes symbolic. Earwicker's guilt stems from an incident which takes place in the park, an actual place known to Earwicker, but the feeling of guilt forces Earwicker's identification with other guilty heroes in history: he becomes for instance, Adam and Tristram who fell through sin. The well-known place changes and the characters do, too, as Earwicker's feelings toward his daughter Isabel are transformed into feelings of guilt and translated into the love-relationship between Tristram and Iseult.

Earwicker, moreover, does feel responsible; his guilt is concerned with something sexual as well as something religious, two sources of guilt universal for man. Earwicker himself takes on more strongly the sexual guilt, while his son takes on the religious guilt. But his son is himself; his son's excommunication and trouble with religious leaders becomes his. His sons' sexual accusations are really disguises for his own feelings of guilt over such matters. Shaun, however, warns Isabel, his sister, who is the Church, the enemy of Satan. These opposing principles are fused together in drives, ambitions, and feelings that are greater than any one man or individual. This is another reason for Joyce's development of a cosmic kind of language. The novel is universal because what is spoken of and dreamed of is cosmic. The language expands the particular into the universal.

There are two other forces present in the novel that match the feelings which are spoken of in terms of light and darkness through the characters of Shem and Shaun, and those are the symbols of the river and the hill (the image of Earwicker and his wife, Anna). Often in a dream there is an absence of clear and unambiguous images; the same absence is evidenced here. The blurring together of faces, of personalities, of persons, is true in *Finnegans Wake* to the extent that mere echoes of voices and fragments of personalities are presented. There is, however, one image which crescendos in significance throughout the novel, that is, the vying of opposites in the image of the hill and the river. Anna Livia becomes synonymous with the water and the river. In the Anna Livia Plurabelle section the washerwomen's talking to one another fit into the river's rippling dialogue with itself concerning Anna. She is purgation; she is the source from which the mound extends. The two opposing principles, the vertical mound and the horizontal river together symbolize sexual complements and the beginning of life:

> For I feel I could near to faint away. Into the deeps. Annamores leep. Let me lean, just a lea, if you le, bowldstrong bigtider. Allgearls is wea. At times. So. While you're adamant evar. Wrhps, that wind as if out of norewere! As on the night of the Apophany-pes. Jumpst shootst throbbst into me mough like a bogue and arrohs! Ludegude of the Lashlanns, how he whips me cheeks! Sea, sea! Here, weir, reach, island, bridge. Where you meet I. The day. Remember! (P. 626)

The dreamer of the tale calls forth the light of day and another self

71

through the voice of Anna Livia, who is the sea, the water, and the river. Her voice suggests that we each are islands and incomplete until we find the bridge that is another person, the place "where you meet I," the light, unity, and completion.

Anna Livia's name changes just as do the names of her sons: "Allaniuvia pluchrabelled" (p. 627), "Alma Luvia Pollabella" (p. 619). It is significant that her voice comes in at the end of the book, after "Sandhyas! Sandhyas! Sandhyas!" (p. 593), the threefold call to dawn is heard opening the last section. She is the source, the day, the dawn toward which all darkness and incompletion merge. This prayer-word in Hinduism is said at the most significant changes of time—at dawn, at sunset, and at noon. It indicates the moment which opens to another significant one. Anna's voice echoes this change again as the reader hears her proclaiming dawn: "I wisht I had better glances to peer to you through this baylight's growing. But you're changing, acoolsha, you're changing from me, I can feel. Or is it me is? I'm getting mixed Brightening up and tightening down" (pp. 626–627).

The final meeting of the two principles, the hill and the river is very explicit at the end of the novel: "If I seen him bearing down on me now under shitespread wings like he'd come from Arkangels, I sink I'd die down over his feet, humbly dunbly, only to washup. Yes, tid. There's where" (p. 628). This merging of the hill and the water into a sexual kind of image represents life, completion: in fact, the affirmation after the image is the clue. There is a suggestion of the experience of separation and then union. The sound of the gull reminds the hearer that its voice is calling for the union of the two opposites—the hill and the river—man and woman: "Us then. Finn, again!" (p. 628). The cry, "mememormee," finds its echo and complement in the "Till thousendsthee." The two principles unite and disengage after the exclamation of "Us then. Finn, again!" The union means separation and union again. After the fusion the hill and the river are again alone. They are distinct images: "Away a lone a last a loved a long the ..." (p. 628). They can only be related to a distinctness and loneliness seeking union again through repetition and circularity. For the "the" becomes the word preceding "riverrun, past Eve and Adam's, from swerve of shore to bend of bay, brings us by a commodius vicus of recirculation back to Howth Castle and Environs" (p. 3). The path of the journey from union to disengagement and back to union again is part of the history of man which Vico's cyclical view of history presents. Howth Castle and Environs become "Here comes everybody" and the dreamer's ego

—Humphrey Chimpden Earwicker. He is encircled of course by the river who is Anna Livia.

*Finnegans Wake* is not only a dream, but often a dream within a dream, and a dream within a dream within a dream. While Joyce is dreaming of Earwicker's dream, Earwicker is dreaming of Shem's and Shaun's, and Shaun's voice is heard dreaming of his sister and his brother. Anna Livia is dreaming too. Her voice represents a kind of descant over the final sleeping hours of the whole dream while the dream and the reality of the person become wedded together.

Sleep and the dream are called by the narrator "nonland": "Methought as I was dropping asleep somepart in nonland of where's please (and it was when you and they were we) I heard at zero hour as 'twere the peal of vixen's laughter among midnight's chimes from out the belfry of the cute old speckled church' " (p. 403). While dream is nonland because it is a dimension lacking space and time, waking from the dream confronts the individual with nonidentity. Proust's narrator in *A la recherche du temps perdu* experiences this: "But it was enough that, even in my bed, my sleep was deep enough to entirely relax my spirit. Then my mind could let go of the mere locality where I had gone to sleep, and when I awoke in the middle of the night, since I had no idea where I was, I couldn't even tell, for a moment, who I was."[47] In the dream, the experience of being forces the person to live in "nonland." The sense of personality in a dream is at its lowest while free association and fusion of personalities permit an infinite number of creative possibilities. In his dream Every-man almost becomes a god as the narrator in *Du Côté de chez Swann* indicates: "The sleeping man weaves in a circle about him the thread of hours, the order of years and worlds."[48] Transcending space and time, the dreamer becomes everyone and godlike.

The fact that the dream allows for changes in personality and in time sequences permits the dreamer to see parts of himself as he rewrites history. This could not be done in conscious, rational activity. Shem and Shaun as aspects of Earwicker remain distinct personalities, yet they blur with Earwicker's personality. Disengagement and the union of the hill and river, the signs of Anna and Humphrey, or Adam and Eve, evoke and point to a self which is a composite of tensions, opposites, and circles. In the circle what happens once is repeated. "What will be is. What is is" (p. 620). The future, the present, and the past, the father, the son, daughter and father, husband and wife are all blurred into one personality. The dream ends with the cry that the pilgrimage has been through a circle of self, "mememormee" (p. 628). The "mes" are always incomplete until they are "thees": "Till thousendsthee" (p. 628). The dream weds opposites that unite and disengage: the "Us then. Finn, again!" becomes "alone a last a loved a long the" (p. 628). Union and fusion has taken place so the circle can continue into disengagement and union again. The cries will always be between the hill and the river from the "mememormee! till thousendsthee." The keys have been given. They are to the kingdom of the dream in which the dreamer is a god, creating through his word a new universe.

In conclusion, the dream and what it represents for man evoke the primitive structure of myth. *Finnegans Wake* creates a world in which mythical expression is at its highest level. The narration is a cosmic "epiphany" in Joyce's words, a "dramatic breakthrough of the sacred"[49] in Eliade's, and the *mana* of Cassirer. In addition, as Lévi-Strauss points out, myth mediates between opposites; it reconciles and fuses polarities. *Finnegans Wake* reveals opposing forces in the self and unites them. The heroes of the myth become gods: "The actors in myth are supernatural beings. They are known primarily by what they did in the transcendent times of the 'beginnings.' . . . Myth then is always an account of a creation."[50]

The self rises in the myth of the wake through the Viconian circle which weds creation and creator, dream and dreamer. Yet a circle is always closed; its direction can only be two ways. The labyrinth, two circles locked together, provides additional directions. Between the circle and the labyrinth, however, the gods must be unmasked, new faces and new selves searched.

# 4 / BETWEEN THE CIRCLE AND THE LABYRINTH: MASK, PERSONALITY, AND IDENTITY—LUIGI PIRANDELLO

Certainly one of the problems in defining identity is the relationship between the self and the many masks which are worn for either public or private acceptance. A person or self can have so many masks and so many public poses that at times he questions which one of these is really himself. Is he the sum total of all his masks or is he none of them? Should his real self be identified with his personality, whatever that might be? What part of himself is really "I"? Coming to terms with the nature of mask and personality, then, is very important in any exploration of identity. Central to this search for self, masks and the use of masks in literature are revelations of self. For although persona and mask seem to suggest the hiding of something, they are as much a revelation as a concealment. In the choice of persona and in the enforced use of mask, the self concomitantly yields something. Every choice of a mask eliminates at the same time the use of another.

In drama the mask is very ancient. Beginning as a functional part of the voice apparatus, it took on a significance that went beyond the voice enlargement which the Greek mask provided. The mask became a role in *Comedia dell'arte* where in spite of a more fixed story line, the actor could "freely" respond to the extent that his understanding of the mask he wore allowed and to the extent that he was forced to respond by the masks of others. Luigi Pirandello, a twentieth century playwright, has added a new dimension to the understanding of masks in the theater. As well as illuminating the problem of identity through masks, Pirandello has also said some very significant things about the relationship of art and the self, art and life.

Another aspect of the search for self is that of the author in his works. This, too, Pirandello's use of masks illumines. The extent to which the author is present in the drama of his characters is an artistic problem which offers valuable insights into the nature of identity.

There is also a problem of the meaning of personality in relationship to the mask and self. At times an expression of personality in this context seems to be a definition of what is most stable in oneself. At other times, the self with its many poses is called personality. Personality, moreover, can be understood in two different ways: first, as the sum of all possible judgments about the self; and, second, as the stable core which exists between the public and private life of the self. If understood in the first way, personality is elusive as well as infinite, because there are no boundaries to the number of judgments that a person can make about himself and elicit from others. Any number of masks is possible, depending upon the intensity of the individual's quest for a more adequate container or for more witnesses to his many "selves."

In literature, moreover, as the number of readers multiplies and as different points of view relating to a persona or mask increase, the number of masks increases. This parallels the life of each person outside of literature, for his masks are very much related to the situations he finds himself in and the roles he must perform as well as the functions with which he is identified. In other words, each reader or person creates masks for others as the result of his judgment. There are, in addition, the judgment on the self by the subject or author and the concomitant judgments of himself by his readers or his beholders. These multiple viewpoints of the subject and the reader are epistemological factors which enter into the open-ended nature of persona as well as the elusiveness of personality.

The manner in which the judgments of others create different selves is very forcefully brought out in the play *Così è (se vi pare)* by Luigi Pirandello. Although in the passage which follows the judgments of people do not relate directly to personality, they do illustrate the manner in which the judgment of witnesses affect the multiplicity of selves and consequently identity. The townspeople are confused as to the identity of Signora Ponza. Some think she is the daughter of Signora

Frola, others that she is the wife of Signor Ponza. Finally at the end of the play she reveals this mystery about the truth of her identity:

SIGNORA PONZA : (*speaking slowly and distinctly*)—what? the truth? it is simply this: that I am, yes, the daughter of Signora Frola—

ALL (*with a sigh of satisfaction*) :—ah!

SIGNORA PONZA : (*rapidly*)—and Signor Ponza's second wife—

ALL (*stupefied and disappointed, in an undertone*) :—Oh! What's this?

SIGNORA PONZA : (*rapidly*)—yes; and as for myself, no one! no one!

THE PREFECT : Ah, no; as for yourself, madam, you must be one or the other!

SIGNORA PONZA : No, gentlemen. Where I'm concerned, I am she whom you believe me to be.

> *For a moment she looks at all of them. Then she exits. Silence.*

LAUDISI : So then, gentlemen, this is the voice of truth!

> *He looks around with contemptuous defiance.*

Are you satisfied?

> *He breaks out laughing.*[1]

Signora Ponza's reply, "I am she whom you believe me to be," is an excellent expression of the way in which the epistemological value of another's judgment creates a different self. To call the result of the creation a new personality of the individual would be too pretentious, since the phenomena of the person remain stable while the interpretations of the phenomena are many. The quest for truth is another aspect of this play; the mask is not the truth about the person but simply the appearance of it. Here the projections of the other, of the viewer, create masks of the viewed. To a large extent the reader is projecting as well as the author. The person has an infinity of masks to cope with as he becomes more aware of the judgments which cause these different selves.

In this play Laudisi becomes the *raisonneur* of Pirandello. He is more or less the unsubtle mask of the author. As his characters struggle to maintain their truth against the projected masks of the viewer and beholder, the author very directly states his opinions concerning the whole conflict through the voice of Laudisi. At one point in the play Laudisi tells the gossipmongers that documents would perhaps satisfy them as to the identity of Signora Ponza. He, however, could not be satisfied with documents because truth is not found in the outside. He claims that he can penetrate the mind of another only through what the other says of himself: "I? But I'm being very careful not to deny anything! You, not I, need data, facts, documents, to affirm or deny! I stay out of that, because for me reality does not consist in such things, but in the mind of those two people, into which I know I cannot enter unless they allow me to."[2] While the people of the town are busily intent about discovering the truth, he assures them that things are not absolutely true or false but they are true depending upon a point of view. He insists on this with Signora Sirelli: "Ah, no, madam, I think this is where you are wrong! Where your husband is concerned, rest assured things are as he tells you they are."[3]

One of the most significant moments in the play is the experience Laudisi shares with the audience while staring into the glass. He manages to see his reflection in the glass and ponders his image as he sees it and the distance between that which is his image of himself and others' image of him while all are reflected and refracted in the curve of the glass:

> LAUDISI (*He walks around the studio a bit, groaning to himself and shaking his head; then he stops in front of the big mirror on the mantlepiece, looks at his face and says*) :
> Oh, there you are!
> *He waves a hand in greeting, winks an eye archly and laughs.*
> Well, friend, which of the two of us is crazy?
> *He points a finger at himself in the glass, and his reflection points back at him. He laughs again, then:*
> Yeah, I know: I say "you" and you point back at me. We certainly know one another well. It's a shame that the rest don't see you as I do. Well then, friend, what's going to happen to you? I have you here in front of me, I can see you and touch you. But the way the rest see you—what will you become for them? A phantasm, friend, pure phantasm. Well, you see these crackpots? They have no idea of the phantasms they carry around inside themselves, and go running like crazy into other people's phantasms. And they think it's something else.
> *The butler enters and stops in astonishment as he hears Laudisi speaking the last words to the mirror.*[4]

Interestingly enough, the stage directions are for the butler to come into the room and view Laudisi as Laudisi is viewing himself in the glass. The number of viewers is multiplied here and in a very telling moment shows the forceful power of the many possible projections. Laudisi, watching himself, is being watched by the audience, who are watching the butler and Laudisi observing himself. The number of images, projections, and masks always seems so open-ended that the person is never adequately defined by any one of his viewers. Since each viewer has a different projected mask or a different projected image of the other and since the viewed has his own image of himself which is partially the result of the projected masks of the other and also his own projections and insights of himself, he never is totally content with all these different poses as being his explanation.

Another play that significantly develops the function of the mask and identity is *Enrico IV*. *Enrico IV* weds the mask and history to the theme of madness. While Enrico is contemplating the past and the madness that people have projected on him even when he ceased to be mad, he fiercely delivers the following: "But tell me, could you be quiet if you knew there was someone going around trying to persuade people that you are what he thinks you are, trying to get them to form their opinion of you according to his judgment?—'Madman' 'madman'!"[5] Here Enrico insists that one person's projection is not absolute for others. There are, in other words, many possible interpretations of who a person is. Consequently, he decries in this speech words and labels: "Crush a man with the weight of a word? That's nothing. What is it? A fly. All of life is like that—crushed by the weight of words! The weight of the dead."[6] Here words and labels are categories by which the mask is fossilized and the person no longer is himself. This evil use of the mask is decried by Enrico who knows that he is wearing a mask. His mask is that of feigned madness because he ceased to be mad long ago. After an "accident" he lost his memory and thought that he was really Enrico IV. Since he was dressed up as him in the masquerade, he lived this life of Enrico IV and became frozen in time. The mask in this function escapes history and time. As someone fixed by an historical event, Enrico IV never grew old. He then consciously kept this mask of madness even when it no longer was significant for him. To his courtiers in the mad palace, Enrico IV vacillates between madness and sanity. He lashes out at them for their interpretation of his plight. He tries to convince them that what they see is their own construction. In all of these conflicts the tension between the truth and the illusion, between the

person and the mask, between history and time, madness and identity
are revealed as components of the construct called self. Enrico's terrible
cry is that the label "mad" which was foisted upon him was the unsym-
pathetic lack of recognition of the person as he really was. This, he said,
drove him to a feigned insanity which was both a torture and an escape:

> I would hate you to suffer as I have in thinking of this horrible
> thing, which really drives one mad: that you were alongside some-
> one and looking into his eyes—as I one day looked into someone's
> eyes—imagine that you were a beggar standing before a door
> through which you could never enter: whoever might enter, it
> would never be you with your own inner world that you can see
> and touch; but someone unknown to you would see you and touch
> you, someone with his own impenetrable world.[7]

Once the person becomes the construction of another, once Enrico becomes the construction of his family, the real Enrico becomes changed
and actually the creation of the other. Aware of this, Enrico is also
conscious of how his masquerading as a character of history transcends
and escapes time:

> And to think that at a distance of eight centuries from us, from
> this remote age of ours with all its light and darkness, the men of
> the twentieth century will battle and struggle in restless anxiety
> trying to understand the meaning of their fate, to see through the
> maze of events that keep them in such distress and agitation.
> Whereas you are already in history! with me![8]

History, like art, has a certain amount of immutability about it. What
has happened can never un-happen in time. What has become fixed
(*fissati per sempre*) and frozen in art and history never ages. The past
is already known, the present and the fate of a person in the present and
the future is constantly changing, constantly shifting. In actuality time
is more a dream, more an illusion than art or the historical event. Here
the symbol of the character in history and his mask becomes a symbol
which weds him to history as well as art. It transcends the mutable
quality of time and becomes the symbol of the unchanging and the
transcendent. Enrico refuses even at the end of the play to be the unconscious construction of another. While claiming that all of us wear masks,
he wears his consciously. We are the construction of others, he insists,

but we also choose our own masks without the full realization that we are doing so. He, at least, is aware of this:

> We have to pardon them! This,
>> *he touches his costume*
> this is for me the external and voluntary symbol of that other continual masquerade, the one that goes on all the time, in which we are the involuntary actors
>> *points to Belcredi*
> when without knowing it we mask ourselves with what we think we are. Forgive them this costume of theirs: they do not yet see that it is identical with themselves.[9]

The tragic thing about the mask, he claims, is that while worn unconsciously, it becomes identical with the person. When the mask is understood as being distinct from the person, as something which escapes time, it becomes a form of art.

Personality is another dimension of the mask. It is the concretization of all the inarticulate feelings and projections of the mask. Personality transcends the mask, however, since it can also be understood as the more stable part of the self which is present in many of the masks and shines forth through the holes in the eyes of the mask. As the eyes become that part of the person through which a lie cannot be told, the mask loses its impregnability. The personality of a person is like his eyes which, although they may feign and pretend, reveal a truth deeper than the person is willing to express.

While *Enrico IV* speaks directly of history and the mask as being frozen in time, *Sei personaggi in cerca d'autore* shows the immutability of a person in art. It also communicates valuable insights on the nature of personality. Here the author, or rather the personality of the author, is also very significant since his own persona and mask is the creator of the masks of his characters. Pirandello, in addition, is very much preoccupied with the tension between reality and illusion as well as how this conflict relates to the many selves of every individual.

The ties between persona, personality, and character are very close. Through the character of a play Pirandello often articulates his own search. Sometimes the expressions are projections of aspects of his own self and, consequently, very close to the nature of the mask of the creator. His own personality is hidden behind the masks which the characters present to others. In fact, it seems in his universe that regardless of how denuded of their masks his characters are, they still find communication impossible. For the characters can only reveal themselves through words which are inadequate to explain their deepest feelings and their most profound pain. Not even the author understands them because, although they were born in his fancy, they remain a mystery to him. Pirandello suggests this in his preface to *Sei personaggi in cerca d'autore:*

> Could such an author ever tell how and why a character took shape in his imagination? The mystery of artistic creation is the same as the mystery of natural birth. A woman in love can desire to become a mother; but the desire alone, no matter how intense, can never suffice. One fine day she will find herself a mother, without a precise indication of when it happened. Thus also a living artist receives many seeds of life in himself and yet he can never say why and how, at a certain moment, one of these life-bearing seeds is inserted into his imagination to become a new creature, living on a level of life far above the talkative existence of every day.
>
> I can only say that without having precisely sought them, I found myself in the presence of these six characters, as alive as if I could touch them and hear the sound of their breathing.[10]

In fact, after having created them this way, Pirandello tried to rid himself of them. But he could not. They were dreamed up by him and now had a separate reality: "The truth is that although I persistently tried to blot them out of my mind they continued to live on their own. It was as though they were completely detached from every narrative context, like characters from a romance, miraculously stepping out of the pages of a book" (p. 15). Consequently, characters conceived as different objectified aspects of the author's creative self need a play. Pursued by his characters, Pirandello, the creator, ironically needs them and can only be exorcised of them by incorporating them into a play. The relationship between the mask and the creator, then, is particularly important here. The maker and his relation to the mask is a significant dimension in the exploration of the self.

The *personaggi* in Pirandello's play *Sei personaggi* have become so independent of their maker that they seem to be good examples of this creation exploration. Even Pirandello, their author, is awed by their reality:

> They are removed from me; they live by themselves, with their own

voices and movements. Hence they have become themselves through their struggle against me for their own life. They are dramatic characters, characters that can move and speak for themselves. They already see themselves in this way. They have learned how to defend themselves against me, and they will learn how to defend themselves against others. (P. 16)

Not only are these characters independent of their author, they are part of him. What Pirandello rejects in them is their drama, the tension that arises from their interaction: "Now you must understand what it is I have rejected in them: not the characters themselves, evidently, but rather their drama, which doubtless was of supreme interest to them, but in fact held no interest for me, as I have already indicated" (p. 18).

Although Pirandello accepts these characters into his fancy he will not accept their drama and, therefore, they must search for another author. It seems as if Pirandello sees them as aspects of himself, and yet wants these objectified aspects to find an author for their drama. For in their quest they will also bring him deeper insight into his own self. Their drama becomes his once they are free to search: "I have opened myself to the realization of these six characters: but they come to me already rejected: in search of another author" (p. 18). Through their incorporation into art, the author becomes eternal in the permanence of his characters:

So it is that whenever we open the book, we find Francesca alive and confessing her gentle sin to Dante; and if we go back and read that passage a hundred thousand times, Francesca will speak her lines a hundred thousand times in a row, never with mechanical repetition, but saying them every time as though it were the first time, and with such vivid and spontaneous passion, that once again, as for the first time, Dante will faint away. (P. 22)

Here the problem of personality and relationship to mask once stated by Pascal becomes the touchstone of Pirandello's explorations: "There is no man who differs more from another than he does from himself at another time."

The usually mentioned tension by critics between illusion and reality is very much on the surface in the plays of Pirandello. It is very subtly linked to epistemology since the persona is viewed by many knowing subjects. In one sense the persona becomes multiplied according to the judgments of the perceiver. The important question to be discussed here, then, is which is the true reality of the person? Is he the sum total of the judgments of others or does he have a constant and fixed reality? The father in *Sei personaggi* articulates the problem very well: "And yet we have the illusion, in every act of ours, that we are always "once and for all," and always "just this one." It is not true, not true!"[11] The father insists that we are more than we are in one act, and it would be false to define a person by the perspective of one situation:

> This becomes evident, when, in any one of our acts, to take a very uncomfortable example, we are suddenly, as it were, plucked up and suspended in thin air. We become aware, I mean, of not being totally ourselves in that action, and hence that it would be an atrocious injustice to be judged in that alone, to be plucked up and pilloried in that way for our whole existence, as though our existence could be totally summed up in that action! (Pp. 55–56)

The father's anguished cry, here, is that he does not want his real self to be mistaken for one of his personae. He is more than one of his poses.

Moreover, the fact that personality is not exhausted or identified by the judgments of others is complicated by the person's own perspective of himself. This too the father suggests is illusory:

> Very well, sir: think again of those illusions you no longer cherish, of all those things which no longer "seem" as they "were" for you. Don't you feel the loss, not so much of theatrical images, but of the very ground under your feet? "This" thing that you experience now, today, all the reality of it as it is, is destined quite simply to appear to you tomorrow as pure illusion. (P. 95)

Because of these many obstacles real communication between people, the father observes, is rarely achieved: "We think we understand one another; we never do" (p. 48).

Yet the father is not always Pirandello's spokesman. Each character has his own tragic story: the story of one fuses so completely with the other that the tragedy of each is the tragedy of all. They are not only searching for an author to explain them, but they feel that the meaning of each is related to explaining the other. The tragedy is such a shared one that the characters need to act it out over and over again before one another in the futile hope that the play or story itself will reveal their meaning to themselves. This is the reason why Pirandello "betrays himself" when he suggests in his preface that he is interested in these personae as characters but not their drama. For their drama, the tension among them, is what makes clear to them who they are. It is through their drama and interaction that the author understands these aspects of his own personality better.

Yet even in this search the characters have a permanence which the author or director cannot have. As Pirandello states very early in his preface, this is true because the personae as characters are frozen as images of art. The stage directions too emphasize the immutability of the *personaggi* over the "reality" of the actors:

> Characters must not appear as phantasms, but as created realities, built out of the immutable imagination, and so more real and consistent than the speaking naturalness of the actors. The masks help to give the impression of a figure created by art and serve to fix each character in the immutable expression of his own fundamental sentiments, remorse for the Father, vengeance for the stepdaughter. (P. 35)

Consequently, the search for identity through the use of personae reveals a further insight because of artistic permanence. For once an author has chosen to express himself through different personae, these aspects of his reality retain a stability and permanence beyond himself. The playwright as well as the novelist or poet can look at these personae and proclaim: "I am in all of them." Yet each is only a stage on his life's path because they remain the same in art while the author's fancy gives birth to new personae, new characters, and new drama. The words of the father quoted above agree with Pirandello's statement on Dante: characters and personae are more real than the author himself. Perhaps this is the reason for the inversion in the play: the *personaggi* have reality. It is the author whose reality is so fugitive that it cannot be found in any one play, situation, voice, or character. Cantoro observes this about the illusiveness of personality in Pirandello: "In a word, you arrive at a hundred thousand (and more) 'I's' not only because a hundred thousand individuals can know me, 'each in his own way,' but also because each one of them will form a different concept of me depending upon the moment in which he considers me."[12] If this statement is conceded, every reader becomes a persona, judging the characters, envying their permanence.

Consequently, the I must be distinguished from its myth. *The I must be distinguished from the stories that it tells about itself,* as well as from the stories that others foist upon it. Since the myth of the I is the creation of the other who views the I, it is a fiction or construction. Hence the I is not one but one hundred thousand. The I becomes no one because the origin of the hundred thousand always eludes self:

> And so I removed myself a thousand miles from its creation, and perhaps also from my own, the one I made for myself.—Thus I will never be "one," neither for myself nor for others, even if I and all the rest think that I am "one." On the contrary, I will always be "no one," because the true origin of all those "hundred thousand" I's will always escape me as well as the rest.[13]

Cantoro further observes that there is a dynamic quality in personality. The I behind the many personae, he claims, does not *consist* of diverse elements but *becomes*. Personality becomes, changes from moment to moment, never remains the same, while the character of persona, fixed in art, lives the moment eternally: "Thus, personality does not "consist" in this or that, but "becomes," in me as in every other man. My personality, in someone else's mind, will vary from moment to moment not only because my own concept of myself varies in me, but because every other man's varies in him."[14]

Lawrence Durrell in *The Alexandria Quartet* uses relativity of perspective in time and place as the basis of his thesis on person. In *Balthazar* Pursewarden is quoted as saying that our whole lives are constructions: " 'We live' writes Pursewarden somewhere, 'lives based upon selected fictions. Our view of reality is conditioned by our position in space and time—not by our personalities as we like to think. Thus every interpretation of reality is based upon a unique position. Two paces east or west and the whole picture is changed.' "[15]

While the quartet itself could be used as a study on the nature of mask, personality, and the relativity of every judgment, and consequently the relativity of every mask and every self in space and time, the following comments will be the limit of the discussion here. Lawrence Durrell's characters, like Pirandello's, are obsessed with the relativity of truth based upon the limit of every epistemological judgment, even self-judgment. For instance, Balthazar exclaims: "A diary is the last place to go if you wish to seek the truth about a person" (*Balthazar,* p. 15). It seems that even the words of a diary are the mask of the author and the self. This thought will be particularly developed in the chapter on *Les Faux-Monnayeurs* wherein Edward, the novelist, keeps a diary as Gide, the chief creator, is writing his diary of *Les Faux-Monnayeurs* and his personal diary, his journals.

Since masks can be and are multiple constructs of the self as well as of the other selves or witnesses, personality is illusive, as Mountolive in *Balthazar* exclaims: "Personality as something with fixed attributes is an illusion" (*Balthazar*, p. 15). New data and new facts are not necessarily the answer to the problem of truth. This is the key to understanding the method of Lawrence Durrell in *The Alexandria Quartet*. The mask is the unique way of achieving permanence and some type of immutability either in art or in life which makes the problem of the illusiveness of the mutable personality insignificant. The self knows he is more than his poses but at least he has a pose to witness his existence, his self, in private and in public. The real self, of course, is beyond personality and mask, it is not yet. Pursewarden realizes this and is quoted on this point in *Clea*: "There is no Other; there is only oneself facing forever the problem of one's self-discovery!" (*Clea*, pp. 98–99).

Finally, persona, character and personality are all aspects of the self who dreams, who creates them. And all of these are on a moving scale. For as persona, character, and personality evolve and change, the self who creates them from fancy becomes other than he was at the time of creation. While ontologically the personality or self of the author seems to be the stable element, it is the opposite artistically. Artistically the characters, the personae, are real while the author who is a person as well as a personality is elusive and unreal. His real self is found more in the characters of his fancy, the phases of his dream, than it is in the self he believes is responsible for them. The image of Pirandello's characters dancing before his mind, haunting him until he gives them reality and permanence, is a magnificent articulation of how persona, through character, lives beyond the personality of the dreamer. The personality of anyone, consequently, is as contingent and relative as are his many poses; art makes the contingent permanent and endows it with the quality of necessity. The mask now is the composite construction of the viewer as well as the viewed. Paradoxically, it is further from the reality of the self than personality; yet through art, history, and consciousness, the mask reveals another self which transcends the present and fixes it with a name. The mask, the creator's as well as the created's other self, encourages self-definition as well as rebukes it for its inadequacy and pride.

## Circles Without Center

When Quentin and Miss Rosa in *Absalom, Absalom!* seek to re-create the real Sutpen and when the characters in *The Alexandria Quartet* seek the real truth, they in fact are forming constructs of others as well as of themselves. These constructs have a defining type of energy on the creator himself. Quentin sees this in his retelling of the Sutpen story to Shreve as he wonders whether Sutpen's image shaped all of them in never ending circles of time, never totally confining circles of selves:

> Maybe happen is never once but like ripples maybe on water after the pebble sinks, the ripples moving on, spreading, the pool attached by a narrow umbilical water-cord to the next pool which the first pool feeds, has fed, did feed, let this second pool contain a different temperature of water, a different molecularity of having seen, felt, remembered, reflect in a different tone the infinite unchanging sky, it doesn't matter: that pebble's watery echo whose fall it did not even see moves across its surface too at the original ripple-space, to the old ineradical rhythm . . .[16]

In Quentin's words the ripples of the pool move outward, causing the same movements in a nearby pool. The pools, like circles of selves or people linked sometimes by the narrowest of ties, exercise a mutual effect on each other. The ripples reaching ever beyond the mysterious center into newer circumferences and horizons form labyrinths of relationships. The two pools like two interlocking circles form a labyrinth whose center seems to have disappeared but whose presence is always felt.

# 5 / THE MYTH OF THE LABYRINTH AND
# THE SELF

The myth of the labyrinth has very ancient roots. It finds one of its earliest poetic statements in the *Metamorphoses* of Ovid. Since Ovid, the myth has been retold in a variety of settings. In fact, contemporary literature is replete with resonances of the myth. Modern man seems to find the labyrinth an accurate metaphor for himself and the world in which he lives. Each retelling of the story is an attempt at an explanation of the meaning of the myth. If Gide, for instance, changes the story, he does so for very definite reasons and the changes themselves involve an interpretation of the myth. In addition to Gide's rather direct retelling of the myth, many other writers in contemporary fiction have used elements of it. The maze, the search, the fear and inability of man to find his way out of problems are elements of the labyrinthine myth which are often submerged in the "story" line. They are used to point out and illustrate some of the more profound questionings of modern man on the nature of his identity.

As man seeks meaning both inside and outside himself, he finds that the labyrinth mirrors both aspects of his search. Like the Greeks who discovered that the gods were dead and the universe chaotic and maze-like, modern man wants to understand himself in terms of the myth. Perhaps the energy underlying the myth and its retelling comes from the fact that man's search for self becomes labyrinthine as he proceeds. The following chapter outlines the main features of the myth and later applies the displaced elements to the retelling of the myth in modern

89

literature. Since man's search for self becomes labyrinthine, the nature of labyrinth will be explored with the possibility that man may be himself the labyrinth which often challenges his exploration and which first appears to be outside himself.

In the eighth book of the *Metamorphoses,* Ovid tells the story of the labyrinth and continues it with that of Daedalus and Icarus. Although the two stories are distinct, there is a strong bond between them. Certainly, the obvious connection between the labyrinth as the creation of Daedalus, his eventual imprisonment in it, and his escape from it are explicit bonds, but there are even more subtle links.

In Ovid's story the reason that the labyrinth is constructed is to house the half bull, half man, son of Parsifae, the wife of Minos. Wishing to conceal the shame that came from this monstrous birth, Minos seeks out Daedalus, the great architect, to build something to imprison the monster. Daedalus builds such an intricate series of rooms within rooms, encircled by streams that even he, the architect, the creator, is puzzled about the deceptive paths before him.[1]

Every year Athenian youths are sacrificed, and the demands of the monster increase to such an extent that Theseus, a young Athenian youth, son of Aegeus, decides to rid the world of this monster. Theseus enters the labyrinth and is able to escape by following the thread of Ariadne who loves him. Yet, after Theseus kills the minotaur and escapes the labyrinth, he abandons Ariadne on the island of Dias where Bacchus takes her as his bride. The story of the labyrinth continues with a concentration on the architect, the creator of the labyrinth. The secret of the labyrinth is so subtle, not even its creator could escape. In fact, Daedalus tells his son, Icarus, with whom he is imprisoned in the labyrinth, that neither earth nor water are possible routes of escape. Daedalus confesses to Icarus that only the air is free:

> Daedalus, too long in exile and yearning to see his native sun, exclaimed to Icarus: "Although Minos rules both land and sea, a path still remains for us—the air is free!" And so the creative Daedalus called forth crafts unknown to man.[2]

The pair plan their escape through the construction of a bird-like apparatus of feathers held together by wax. Filled with excitement and the attraction of the heights, the boy, Icarus, flies so high that the wax from his wings melts. He cries out for help from his father but to no avail.[3] Daedalus seeks Icarus unsuccessfully and mourns the death of his son. The story of the labyrinth consequently tells of two escapes: the escape of Theseus with the help of Ariadne and that of Daedalus through waxen wings. All other attempts prove fatal and consequently unsuccessful.

Edith Hamilton retells the story from Ovid and Apollodorus. In her version Theseus is accompanied by other youths from Athens as he makes his way through the labyrinth, and they all escape. She also adds that Ariadne dies, since a violent wind has taken her boat out to sea.[4] The few contradictions and many versions of the story do not alter the basic theme of the labyrinth as the house of a monster—a maze whose ways are so intricate that it can only be overcome by Ariadne's thread and the subtle creativity of its architect.

## A PHILOSOPHICAL INTERPRETATION OF THE MYTH

Among the many explanations of the myth, philosophy has also attempted its explication. One philosopher claims that the story of Ariadne, Theseus, Daedalus, and the Minotaur is a philosophical myth. He explains the myth in terms of the triumph of man's reasoning ability:

> The myth of Ariadne, Theseus, Daedalus, and the Minotaur is a philosophic myth because it deals with man whose understanding leads him from what he feared was chaotic to what he knows to be orderly. It is the myth of all discovery—the guiding image of the courage of reason to overcome fear, ignorance, and superstition.[5]

Paul Kuntz gives his interpretation of the myth in this way: he claims that after Theseus reaches the center of the labyrinth he discovers that there is nothing in it, that the Minotaur is just fiction. Moreover, he has Daedalus tell Theseus that the tunnels are constructed with perfect regularity. Consequently, every succession of turns has a symmetry which reason and logic could easily meet. His conclusion is based on the intelligibility of all reality: "The secret of the labyrinth is that an order may look confusing because people have never thought about its pattern. All patterns are intelligible, and everything has a pattern. Overcome the fear, find the method, the problem gets solved."[6]

In this interpretation, man can overcome the mazes and winding corridors of the labyrinth through his use of reason and understanding. The Minotaur, the monster, does not exist. Daedalus tells Ariadne the secret of the labyrinth—its rational pattern, and its nonexistent monster—so that her lover, Theseus, can escape. With the ball of thread which Ariadne gives him, Theseus finds his way out to safety. Consequently, Theseus kills the fear of the monster through his rational escape engineered by Daedalus and Ariadne. This retelling and explaining of the story is a rather naive one. Its coherence derives from the philosopher's assumption that everything is explainable, that reason can figure out and solve most of man's problems. The labyrinth is a symbol of the barriers to man's understanding. The fear of the Minotaur discourages man, and the fear of the maze prevents him from realizing that he can solve the problems, the riddles, and the chaos of life through his reason and through his confrontation with logical patterns. This interpretation, however, permits reason an omnipotence that man in contemporary literature finds incredible.

Men of letters have groped with the impotency of reason many times. One very graphic illustration of the limitations of reason is that of the labyrinth of purgatory. Here the reader finds Virgil leading Dante through the maze of purgatory in an attempt to identify the evils and problems of the world and in the anxious search for self-identity. But reason has its limits, and Virgil can only lead Dante so far. Beatrice, the symbol of divine love and divine knowledge, must take over and lead Dante through the maze to final vision. The reader can see in the character of Beatrice the necessity for something other than reason in the search for meaning and self-identity. Meaning, consequently, is the result of more than what reason allows and comes from the depths of man, beyond logical inquiry. Ariadne's thread is not as unnecessary as this telling of the philosopher's tale seems to indicate. The point is that, without Ariadne's thread and the symbol for which it stands, man is alone in the labyrinth.

## *THÉSÉE*—ANDRÉ GIDE

André Gide's *Thésée* is similar to the Ovid story as well as significantly different.[7] Gide remains faithful to the essentials of the story, however: Theseus, an Athenian youth, is helped by Ariadne's thread to kill the Minotaur and find his way out of the labyrinth. The obvious differences are found in the chronology. In the Ovid story the chronology seems to indicate that Daedalus and Icarus attempted their escape after Theseus had slain the Minotaur. In Gide's narration it seems that the Minotaur was killed by Theseus after Daedalus and Icarus had escaped from the labyrinth. In fact, Gide has Daedalus give advice to Theseus on the nature of the labyrinth. Even Icarus is on hand to tell his version of the nature of the labyrinth.

It is perhaps illuminating to begin an exploration of André Gide's understanding of the myth and its meaning for man with a study of its creator, Daedalus, and his message to Theseus. Daedalus tells Theseus that perhaps the best way of constructing the labyrinth to house the Minotaur was to make it such that a person would not want to get out. Daedalus claims that no prison, no ditch, no barrier, is impregnable. Consequently, the only foolproof labyrinth is the one which the wanderer does not want to leave:

> Now, since there is no prison that can hold back someone who is really determined to escape, and no barrier or ditch which courage and determination cannot surpass, I thought that the best way to keep someone in the labyrinth was to construct it in such a way that a person would not be so much unable (be sure to grasp my meaning well) as unwilling to get out. Hence I brought into the place things that I knew would satisfy all kinds of appetites.[8]

Daedalus decides to make this labyrinth one whose attractions and pleasures so numb the wanderer that he becomes mystified and seduced by the charm of the labyrinth. Thus, man would not want to get out. He would become more interested in the labyrinth itself than in exiting from it. Whereas it starts out as the means to discovery, the labyrinth becomes an end in itself. In such a setting man obviously loses the sense of his destination, his goal.

Daedalus tells Theseus, moreover, that the perfumes of the labyrinth so charm the person that outside reality has no further command or interest for him. The labyrinth's charms not only prevent the discovery for which the labyrinth is simply a setting, a framework, a means, but also inculcates a helpless type of self-imprisonment through the refusal to escape. Daedalus tells Theseus that he must bring Ariadne with him if he is to leave the labyrinth. She, however, cannot even enter the labyrinth, but must remain on the threshold so as not to sniff the vapors and be overcome by its pleasures. Judging from Daedalus' instructions to Theseus, it would seem that, in Gide's understanding, the only way out of the labyrinth is through the assistance of someone who is able to face the labyrinth, face the maze, but who stands on its threshold. He tells Theseus, moreover, that Ariadne is the tangible sign of his link with reality: "Go back to her, or all hope of fulfilling your destiny is gone. This thread will be your link with the past. Go back to it. Go back to yourself" (p. 1433).

Ariadne's thread becomes symbolic of three very important means of an escape from the labyrinth. The thread in the first place is symbolic of duty: "Since will power alone may not be enough (for, as I told you: these aromas will weaken you) I thought of this: bind yourself to Ariadne by a thread, a tangible image of duty" (p. 1433).

He tells Theseus never to break the thread of duty no matter how seductive the labyrinth becomes, for if he does he is doomed. Secondly, it is symbolic of history. The thread symbolizes the past for Theseus and can only help him to future accomplishments by reminding him of his link with his past. (When Theseus founds the modern Athens, he does so because he has a sense of the past, a sense of the mistakes of the state as well as of the successes which history has revealed; he can, consequently, found a state which has learned from its past.)

The thread, symbolic of duty and of the past, has also an important relationship to the self. Daedalus insists that Theseus should go back to the thread, should go back to himself. It is at this point that Gide's interpretation of the myth underscores the relationship of the labyrinth and identity. "Know yourself" was the often repeated Greek motto. And just as Theseus must go through the labyrinth before he can found the new city, so must he discover the thread of duty, a sense of the meaning of the past, and knowledge of himself before he can make his way through the labyrinth: he must know his own prejudices, his own attractions and self-deceits as well as his individuality: "For nothing comes out of nothing, and everything that you will be is based on your past, on what you are at this moment" (p. 1433).

Daedalus's advice to Theseus is more than simply the advice of a creator telling the world about his creation. It is almost a sermon on how man must live if he is going to make his contribution to the world community. Through the labyrinth of self-discovery Theseus, a favorite hero of the Athenians, has to find, meet, and kill the monster within him before he can grow and contribute what is uniquely his.

What Gide is suggesting in the myth is that the labyrinth is not only outside of man, but that it is chiefly within him. He must kill the monster within himself before he can bring himself into wholeness, into clarity of vision. It is interesting that when Theseus does discover the Minotaur it is asleep: "Before me on a flowery terrace of buttercups, poppies, tulips, jonquils and carnations, in a very relaxed position lay the minotaur. He happened to be asleep'' (p. 1439).

Here, as well as in the seductive corridors and vapors of the labyrinth, Theseus has to exert his courage because the monster was no ugly creature; in fact, Theseus exclaimed "the monster was handsome" (p. 1439). Finding the Minotaur beautiful and killing him somehow has symbolic force: Theseus, who becomes every man meeting the monster within, must take the risk of killing something that he doesn't want to give up, something that he knows, intellectually, is the evil, the non-human in him but which he finds so hard to give up and to kill. Theseus's journey is to the inner depths of a person. It most profoundly explores and tries to cure man of his difficulty in really confronting himself.

After Daedalus gives his advice to Theseus, he calls on his son Icarus to speak. Unfortunately, Daedalus says that Icarus does not understand that the labyrinth was within himself:

> Poor dear child, said Daedalus. Since he thought there was no way out of the labyrinth and did not understand that the labyrinth was inside him, I fulfilled his request and made him wings that would allow him to fly away. He thought he would have to escape skyward, because all earthly routes were closed. I was aware of his mystical tendencies and was not surprised at his wish, an unassuaged wish, as you must have become aware while listening to him. Despite my warning, he wanted to fly too high and overestimated his strength. He fell into the sea and died. (Pp. 1435–1436)

Icarus makes the journey to the center of himself and never finds his way out. He does not have Ariadne's thread, the symbol of reality, and becomes lost in speculation. His is an aspiring mind. He is the image of man's disquiet, the image of poetry. Consequently, Daedalus tells Theseus that since hell is merely the re-enactment of what man tries to do and never succeeds to do in life, Icarus is constantly driven to act out his impulse for discovery: "Icarus was, before his birth, and remains after his death, the image of human unrest, of searching, of the flight of poetry, which he bore in his flesh during his short life" (p. 1436).

Icarus continuously asks questions, speculating on the nature of the universe. He is doomed in his death to re-enact the labyrinth of problems and of unanswerable questions. Icarus is a theologian, a philosopher, a man of perpetual unrest and disquiet. He does not realize that these questions are his own constructions, that they are labyrinths of his own making, that they are a part of his own being. He becomes lost in the center of his own creation. In a sense, Gide is true to the Ovid myth in that the labyrinth is so subtle that even its creator, Daedalus, is lost within its limits. Gide's Daedalus, however, is a more omniscient creator, and it is his son who does not realize that each man constructs his own secret passageways and then makes them his prison:

> But what is the purpose behind all of this, God of light? Why so much suffering and striving? Where does it all end? What is the point of it all? Why insist on a rational explanation for everything? Where are we to go if not toward God? But how choose the course? And where to stop? When have the right to say: So be it; this is the end of the search? How arrive at God starting from man? But starting from God, how can I ever arrive at myself? Nevertheless, is it not so that the God who formed me is himself, in like fashion, created by man? It is precisely at the crossroads, at the very heart of this cross, that my spirit longs to be fixed. (P. 1435)

For Icarus these questionings are the product of logic, the result of man's own reasoning. It is logic which Gide shows has its limits. In the philosopher's interpretation quoted above, logic and reason are the way out of the labyrinth, while in the artist's version logic and reason alone enforce imprisonment and answer no questions.

The labyrinth emerges as a symbol of man's search to understand himself. It is a pilgrimage to the center of man. Icarus's search reveals man intellectualizing his problems, evading his feelings and his self. Theseus reveals man finding himself. The labyrinth, moreover, also means God.

God, self, and the labyrinth find many resonances in Jungian psychology.[9] The labyrinth is something within self, Daedalus tells Theseus. It is a mysterious center which is the self's creation; it is self which is both son and father. Miguel Serrano explains how this self, this center, is to be explored and reached, and asks Jung to comment. Jung's insightful response confirms Gide's view of the labyrinth story: "Inasmuch as my main tenet contains nothing more than: Follow that will and that way which experience confirms to be your own, i.e., the true expression of your individuality."[10]

The journey in the labyrinth is a journey within man, and Jung castigates man for wanting to go to the stars instead of wanting to explore himself further. In a sense, Jung's image of modern man is parallel to the symbol of Icarus wanting to leave the labyrinth in flight rather than journeying into the depths of himself:

> Mankind of today is dreaming of interstellar communications. Could we contact the population of another star, we might find the means of learning something essential about ourselves. Incidentally we are just living in a time when *Homo Hominibus Lupus* threatens to become an awful reality, and when we are in dire need to know beyond ourselves. The science fiction about traveling to the moon or to Venus and Mars and the lore about Flying Saucers are effects of our dim, but nonetheless intense need to reach a new physical as well as spiritual basis beyond our actual conscious world. Philosophers and psychologists of the XIXth and XXth Century have tried to provide a *terra nova* in ourselves, that is the "Unconscious." This is indeed a discovery, which could give us a new orientation in many respects. Whereas our fictions about Martians and Venusians are based upon nothing but mere speculations, the Unconscious is within the reach of human experience.[11]

It is interesting to note that Jung sees in man's flight from earth a flight from himself, a flight which highlights speculations and is characterized more by soaring, unfettered reasoning, than by what is available to man through human experience. In this interpretation, today's man becomes the reflection of Icarus: aimless speculations about the nature of the world and God, flight from self and from the labyrinth within.

In Jung's view, the labyrinth, God, the infinite, and the self, find equality. In explaining the significance of the Gnostic ring, Jung tells Serrano that the number eight is a symbol of the infinite, of the labyrinth, and of the road to the unconscious:

> Above it, the face of a woman; below the number 8, which is a symbol of the Infinite, of the labyrinth, and of the road to the unconsciousness. I have changed one or two things on the ring so that the symbol will be Christian. All of these symbols are absolutely alive within me, and each one of them creates a reaction within my soul.[12]

The infinite which is God, the road to the unconscious which is the journey to self, and the labyrinth which is man's construction as well as man himself, are all related so intricately that one can stand for the other. It is with reason in Gide's version, then, that Icarus, while lost within himself, speculates about the infinite, about God within himself. It is again very appropriate that the creator of the labyrinth is capable of being imprisoned in his own creation when he forgets that it is within himself that he must look for the answer. The labyrinth, consequently, in Gide's story, is within man; it is the self.

Although Ariadne holds the thread which provides Theseus with the way out of the labyrinth, the thread can only be half of Theseus's equipment. In fact, since Ariadne wants control over the thread, Theseus has to take the thread from Ariadne decisively:

> She wanted me to give back to her the balls of thread that Daedalus had given me, claiming that it was women's work to wind and unwind them. She said she was especially skilled at it, and that I shouldn't bother. But in fact what she wanted was in this way to remain in control of my fate, and I could never consent to that. I was afraid that, since she couldn't bear to let me out of her sight, she would unwind the thread unwillingly at best, and would probably tug the thread taut and pick up any slack: this would stop me from forging ahead with all my strength. I stood firm, despite her tears (the supreme female argument) knowing full well that if you give them a little finger they will take your whole arm and everything else.[13]

Consequently, Theseus learns from this first interaction how decisive he must be in following all of Daedalus's suggestions and advice. Theseus makes his way into the labyrinth, kills the Minotaur, and escapes with his companions. A great future awaits Theseus, but he first has to overcome self (of which the labyrinth is so clearly a symbol), and has to come to terms with Ariadne. He does not really love her but her sister, Phaedra. It was Phaedra that he took with him to found the modern Athens.

With the boy, Theseus, that he meets at the beginning of the tale, the reader journeys through the labyrinth which represents the wisdom that the man, Theseus, must acquire before he can accomplish his destiny. The tale narrates the progress of this immature boy to wisdom, to self-discovery, and to the founding of a city which represents intelligence and wisdom. Theseus establishes equality as the great characteristic of the city. Personal merit he proclaims the highest value. Athens is not to be ruled by a tyrant but by a government of the people where equality reigns.

Further, Theseus has to confront his friend Pirithoüs. After helping Pirithoüs through the labyrinth, Theseus, in order to carry out his destiny, has to recognize that even friendship has its limits. Pirithoüs, clinging steadfastly to the status quo, eventually has to be sent away, since Theseus believes in progress. The whole myth, in fact, is based on the progress of a man to his destiny:

> From that time on Pirithoüs no longer followed me. When I was young he accompanied me everywhere and was a great help. But I came to understand that the constancy of friendship could prevent progress and even drag us backwards. There is a point beyond which one must travel alone. Since Pirithoüs was sensible I still listened to him, but that's all. He was aging himself, and the man who had once been so enterprising allowed his wisdom to mellow into temperance. His advice was composed exclusively of restraint and limitation.[14]

Since Pirithoüs has succumbed to temperance, restriction, and restraint as his way of life, he no longer is the man of openness. Theseus, however, still believes in progress.

Not only is Athens founded on the vision of Theseus, but it is also protected by the blessing of the old and now wise Oedipus. Oedipus explains and teaches Theseus much about his life. He tells Theseus at the end that he did not previously understand the grandeur of suffering and its pathway to great destiny. That is why he exclaimed, "O darkness, my light!" It is only through his confrontation with himself, in honesty and suffering, that he can bring a blessing upon Athens. His ashes and his bones are the sign of continual blessing upon the city.

Gide's retelling of the myth shows that the search for self unavoidably becomes labyrinthine. Theseus becomes every man, since every man must make his way through the labyrinth within him before there is discovery. Yet this labyrinth is his own construction, his own self, his own infinite. To create the labyrinth is to create one's self, to leave the labyrinth is to discover the mysteries of oneself which go beyond logic and rules. Icarus is lost within himself, within his logic, and within his questionings. Daedalus teaches Theseus that he must courageously avoid the seductions of the labyrinth and keep his destination ever before him. He must make his journey to self-discovery, and from there he must accomplish his destiny. Theseus's great mission is to found the modern Athens. Every man, however, as Jung, too, indicates, must offer his individuality, his uniqueness, to the world. Before making his contribution, however, man must journey through the maze of self-discovery, the journey to the meaning of his uniqueness. Only then can he govern with balance and with wisdom as did Theseus.

Theseus also represents the man of perpetually widening horizons. He is a man who refuses to draw absolutes to the scale of trivial accomplishments. He is the man who, in avoiding self-imprisonment in the labyrinth, avoids the self-imprisonment of prior conclusions and constraints. While Pirithoüs in his old age speaks of restraint, temperance, and restrictions, Theseus, the open-ended man, speaks of progress and refuses to accept the limits of false absolutes. His future is ever opening before him with its infinite possibilities. For this reason, Oedipus, the wise, the blind but yet all-seeing man, can leave his blessing upon the city. Athens, the city of wisdom, is the result: it is the creation of a man who has passed through the labyrinth, through suffering, to wisdom, to intelligence, and to the infinite possibilities which the future unfolds.

## THE ARTIST AND THE LABYRINTH—JORGE LUIS BORGES

Perhaps no modern writer uses the labyrinth as a metaphor for the cosmos outside and inside man and for man's search for identity more frequently than Jorge Luis Borges. Since so many of his tales use the myth and explore its many dimensions, any number of them could be treated here; for our purposes, the following discussion will seek to mirror the essentials of the deceptively infinite labyrinth.

The symbol of the labyrinth in Borges is an organizing myth intended to communicate the tension between cosmos and chaos, reality and the dream, the quest and the goal. In its symbolic force, the labyrinth can be viewed from three perspectives: "The thought of monstrosity stands always as a dramatic overtone, be it in the minds of those who created the labyrinth (that reproach which is almost remorse and that intellectual horror of Homer-Rufus in "The Immortal"), be it in the construction realized, or in the relationship of the architecture to the being enclosed in it."[15]

For Borges, the labyrinth of the world and the labyrinth of the mind mirror each other. In this context Borges claims that "Valéry illustriously personifies the labyrinth of the mind."[16] Borges's esteem came not only from the fact that Valéry was a great searcher for a world construct in the chaos, but that he was the creator of interior labyrinths as well.

"The Library of Babel" tells of man's attempts within the chaos of the world to construct an ordered system. While the library, the symbol of the universe, is eternal, man is not. His system of space and time is but a mere moment of puzzling labor imposed upon the chaos. Through a book written in "a Samoyedic Lithuanian dialect of Guarani, with classical Arabian inflections,"[17] a librarian of "genius" discovers the fundamental laws of the library: he discovers that the library contains every symbol and combination of symbols:

> Everything: the minutely detailed history of the future, the arch-
> angels' autobiographies, the faithful catalogue of the Library,
> thousands and thousands of false catalogues, the demonstration of
> the fallacy of those catalogues, the demonstration of the fallacy of
> the true catalogue, the Gnostic gospel of Basilides, the commentary
> on that gospel, the commentary on the commentary on that gospel,
> the true story of your death, the translation of every book in all
> languages, the interpolations of every book in all books.[18]

Man stands amazed in the tedious circumspection of his labyrinthine world. Then, again, with amazement from the very depths of his being, springs a book, a hope, which seems to lead to the narrator's self-discovery. This hope is a book which contains everything; all the answers to the mystery of the universe: "I pray to the unknown gods that a man—just one, even though it were thousands of years ago!—may have examined and read it" (p. 57). To find this total book which is his goal, the narrator has to make his way through the puzzling architecture of the library; the library is a labyrinth composed of hexagonal galleries, and two closets: "The universe (which others call the Library) is composed of an indefinite and perhaps infinite number of hexagonal galleries ... One of the free sides leads to a narrow hallway which opens onto another gallery, identical to the first and to all the rest" (p. 51).

Furthermore, the library has a spiral stairway, a mirror (which makes man think that the library is not infinite), and two lamps. Like all men who have gone through a library, the narrator proclaims, he, too, imitating the legend of the Man of the Book, searched for the book, the perfect or total book. According to the legend, the Man of the Book had succeeded in finding the "total book," and, subsequently, he himself became the object of quest. Many people squandered their life in search of him and the book: "We also know of another superstition of that time: that of the Man of the Book . . . In the language of this zone vestiges of this remote functionary's cult still persist. Many wandered in search of Him. For a century they exhausted in vain the most varied areas. How could one locate the venerated and secret hexagon which housed Him?" (p. 56).

Not only is the library a labyrinth, then, but the monster symbolized by this book is also housed here. The monster who is the answer, the secret, the symbol of Daedalus, the creator, is the raison d'être of the library. This is the reason the narrator must search him out and reveal him. Once he is revealed, the labyrinth has no raison d'être other than itself; once Daedalus is released from his prison, the labyrinth has given up its secret. Consequently, while searching for the monster, the book of books, the total book, the creator is searching for the meaning of his existence. All of these are clues to his identity, an identity which is never discovered in this library, but one which is founded on hope: "If an eternal traveler were to cross it in any direction, after centuries he would see that the same volumes were repeated in the same disorder (which, thus repeated, would be an order: the Order). My solitude is gladdened by this elegant hope" (p. 58).

The narrator is alone; he will continue to search, however, because of the hope of finding the total book and the man of the total book. The hope of finding this man who has examined the total book and who could explain the riddle of the circular labyrinths around men urges him on.

As in most of Borges's tales, the context of reality in this nightmarish labyrinth is brought about by his great fidelity to detail. The form of the labyrinth becomes the form of the story. The content contains fictive names as well as real ones. Side by side, the fictive and the real coexist so that the reader, in making his way through the maze of this story as well as through the others, realizes that Borges is smiling. The reader sometimes is trapped in the labyrinth by his own serious identification with the almost ludicrous narrator, searching for the secret of the Library hidden in the book of books.

The relationship between the creator and the creation, Daedalus and his labyrinth, has an important bearing on the form of narration of Borges's short stories. The conflict between the fictive and the real relates to the tension between the narrator and his tale, the narrator trapped in the labyrinth, the reader's identification with the narrator, and, consequently, his own imprisonment in the maze. For instance, the

I of "The Immortal" dreams of the labyrinth again and again since the center of labyrinth means water and life: "Intolerably, I dreamt of an exiguous and nitid labyrinth: in the center was a water jar; my hands almost touched it, my eyes could see it, but so intricate and perplexed were the curves that I knew I would die before reaching it."[19]

Moreover, the relationships between the nightmare and the labyrinth, as well as between vertigo and the labyrinth, are tensions which appear very often in Borges. Repeatedly, fatigue, futility, and search emerge through the narrator's quest for the meaning of self. For instance, before reaching the city of the immortals, the narrator has to pass through labyrinths: "I went down; through a chaos of sordid galleries I reached a vast circular chamber, scarcely visible. There were nine doors in this cellar; eight led to a labyrinth that treacherously returned to the same chamber; the ninth (through another labyrinth) led to a second circular chamber equal to the first."[20]

Immortality for the narrator means the possibility of being everyone and no one, like Odysseus. Like Daedalus, moreover, he betrays himself as he creates, giving little clue to the reader. In "The Immortal" the form of the tale is the answer. Any interpretation which insists on reducing the search to a metaphysical quest while ignoring the artistic implications which form demands, is not seeing any of what the narrator is saying about the tale itself being the labyrinth. When the reader comes in contact with the literary figure of the labyrinth, the anguish of the character's telling of the tale becomes the reader's, forcing the labyrinth to challenge the reader's existences as well as the narrator's. The reader assimilates the doubtful, or rather, fictive existence of the character. He projects into his own existence the possibility that he, too, is fictive, and that he, too, is the victim. For example, in the short story "The Circular Ruins," the witchdoctor dreams a son and inserts him into reality. Scarcely has the dreamed one taken on existence when the dreamer sees him consumed in flames. As he watches the son dissolve, the witchdoctor also realizes that he, too, is evaporating; he, too, has been dreamt up by another; he, too, is fictive: "But they did not bite into his flesh, they caressed him and engulfed him without heat or combustion. With relief, with humiliation, with terror, he understood that he too was a mere appearance, dreamt by another."[21]

In "The Immortal" the reader finds the narrator defining these deceptive paths of the labyrinthine nightmare in the following way: "A labyrinth is a structure compounded to confuse men; its architecture, rich in symmetries, is subordinated to that end."[22] The narrator and the reader are both challenged to find an answer in the labyrinth as the tale is being told. The answer sometimes seems to transcend time, as in "The Garden of Forking Paths." This story traces the search for the identity of the narrator, who is aware that while he is the hunter, he is also, by some ineluctable twist of time, the hunted. The hunter and the hunted coalesce as the narrator pulls the trigger and kills Albert. But just before he pulls the trigger Albert tells him: "Time forks perpetually toward innumerable futures. In one of them I am your enemy."[23] Time itself is the labyrinth forcing the friend to be the enemy, the enemy the friend, the hunter the hunted, and the hunted the hunter. These possibilities seem to obscure the way out of the labyrinth and encourage the "unanimous" feeling the witchdoctor has at the beginning of "Circular Ruins."

If, moreover, as in "Orbis Tertius" a new world that was once discovered and written about will be discovered again, it is only through the mystery of time's labyrinthine and inescapable realities. Time forces the fictive to be considered real and makes the real fictive. The labyrinth and its creator, its creator and the reason for the labyrinth, the monster, somehow all at one time or another converge.

One of the most important elements in the telling of the tale about the creator and his story is that, as he is telling his tale, the storyteller draws his own labyrinth. For instance, in "El Hacedor" Borges claims a creator discovers that while constructing a labyrinth he is tracing the lines of his own face, outlining his own identity.[24] As Borges, the storyteller, weaves his paths through the tale he is creating the other Borges, the storyteller, the one whose identity becomes more real than that of the artist. As in "Sei Personaggi" when the daughter cries out to the director that characters of art have a greater permanence than "real" characters, the storyteller in Borges envies the reality of his fictions. As Pirandello suggests: the artist's characters become even more real than he. Although they are his dreams, they have a reality which transcends his. Borges articulates this in "Borges and I."

Years ago I tried to free myself from him and went from the mythologies of the suburbs to the games with time and infinity, but those games belong to Borges now and I shall have to imagine other things. Thus my life is a flight and I lose everything and everything belongs to oblivion, or to him.

I do not know which of us has written this page.[25]

Borges and his personae, his storytellers, vie for first place in reality. All of them, as in "Everything and Nothing," are "dreams dreamt by many and by no one."[26] The problem of personality and identity is extremely relevant to what Borges is saying. The labyrinth is important as a metaphor for the world and the maze which challenges man's uniqueness; for, while telling the tale, the creator and his form are likewise determined. Form and content are very carefully wedded in Borges's tales. While the content suggests that the universe and man is a maze and that personalities and personal identity are elusive, the form itself proclaims this. The many storytellers of Borges's tales are both hunters and hunted, they are both creators and created.

This exchange of roles suggests the central enigma of the labyrinth myth: the Minotaur, who is the hunted and the reason for the labyrinth, now becomes the hunter, and the creator of the labyrinth in his imprisonment becomes the hunted. This exchange of roles between the traitor and the hero, between the hunter and the hunted, between the witchdoctor and his dreamed son, between the artist and scientist in his third world, at its most profound level is the key to human personality. The personality of an individual, consequently, seems as the masks of Yeats suggest, to be composed of its chief quality and its opposite. But even more, the polarities of roles in human life are brought together and identified by the ironies of time. The traitor does become the friend, the creator does become the created, and the created the creator. The labyrinth remains. It becomes the central clue which allows these shifting identities to be articulated. In the short stories of Borges, the role of the artist, the creator, making his way through his tale, becoming imprisoned in it through his personae, gives him permanence, a permanence and a reality more real than his own personality. His fictions, his labyrinths eventually become him. They trace the image of his own face.

Borges affirms through the paths of his narrations and his tales that man's identity is constantly beckoning him. He becomes paradoxically in time that which he has been hunting. He becomes the hunted as he tries anxiously to recover some traces of his existence. Indeed, Borges is a labyrinth maker whose tales are the form through which the reader manages to have his own personality, identity, selfhood, questioned. In the short parable, "Borges and I," the reader observes that even the creator's personality is challenged by the intruding voice of his narrator. When Borges asks who has told the tale, Borges or I, the reader is reminded of the narrator in "The God's Script," who is in the center of many dreams like the Minotaur in the center of the labyrinth and the author in the center of his fictions: "You have not awakened to wakefulness, but to a previous dream. This dream is enclosed within another, and so on to infinity, which is the number of grains of sand."[27] The exitus from the infinity of dreams is the realization that the self constructs his own labyrinths in his exitus. Man's destiny is to dream, to create within the tale the "other." By this integration Borges seems to point out that a man is every man, while he is in fact no man. He who is both everyone and no one is the author, and the author, who is present everywhere in the expression of his narrators, is really nowhere. He is visible throughout his tale in his characters but he is invisible. Ultimately, this constant identification of the antagonist and the protagonist within the tales blurs the distinction between reality and art.

Borges perfectly exemplifies the literary artist and his labyrinths. He is both Daedalus and the Minotaur, and yet he is neither. For, just as Jung defines personality as a circumference that has no center, the labyrinth seems to be a maze, housing no central meaning. Like the Library of Babel whose circumference is everywhere, its center does not exist. The identification of Daedalus and the Minotaur, the hunter and the hunted, Borges and his narrators, his narrators and characters and readers, form one perfect whole. The labyrinthine paths interweave one upon another. Doors open to other worlds, only to reaffirm that these, too, are labyrinths whose centers are nowhere. The labyrinths have their own raison d'être which transcend content. The form becomes its own reason; the content becomes entirely dependent upon the form. This obliteration of content parallels the identification of hunters and the hunted. Unfortunately, some readers would like to reduce Borges to a metaphysics, since his narrators are raising metaphysical questions. Yet, these questions often deceive the reader into thinking that the content is the only reality, just as the Minotaur suggests that his reality is the raison d'être of the labyrinth. Actually, the labyrinth is its own raison d'être and not the Minotaur. The artist finds these labyrinthine lines tracing the features of his own face, making him everyone and no one, dreamer and the one dreamt, Daedalus and Odysseus (no-one).

## DAEDALUS AND THE NOUVEAU ROMAN—ROBBE-GRILLET

One of the most engaging problems in the literature and theory of the *nouveau roman* is the relationship between subject and object, creator and created, narrator, author, and reader. Critics of Robbe-Grillet insist that man has disappeared from his novels. On the other hand, Robbe-Grillet responds that man has never been more present, particularly in regard to the objects perceived by the narrator. So acutely does he view the intrinsic relationship between subject and object that for him the presence of objects implies the presence of consciously creating subjects. Although he describes objects with great care, Robbe-Grillet maintains that there is always present the *eye* which sees them and the thought which scrutinizes them. In a word, the *objects* in his novels only have presence because of human perspective:

> Man is present in my works on every page and in every line, every word. Even if you also find in them many objects, minutely described, there is always first of all the eye that sees them, thought that scrutinizes them, passion that deforms them. The objects in my novels are never present outside of human perception, real or imaginary. As objects they may be compared to the ones in our daily life much as they hold our attention at every moment.[28]

These objects, moreover, do not have a ready-made signification but are defined in terms of the horizon of the perceiver. What results from the viewpoints of the many perceivers, which include the author, narrators, characters and readers, are many interlocking worlds. Many different worlds emerge from the creative horizons of each of the makers. Robbe-Grillet continues that in a Balzacian universe objects signified something only in relationship to their possessor. Now he claims man no longer believes in fixed significations and a priori meanings for things. Each man, each reader, makes his own meaning; he projects meaning onto the object which he perceives: "We no longer believe in predetermined, ready-made significations which the old divine order handed over to man, as the rationalist order of the nineteenth century did in its turn. Rather we deliver all our hope into man's hands: he alone can create the forms which will bring meaning to the world."[29]

Since man no longer sees himself as a mere namer of objects but as one who gives them gratuitous meaning, the new novelist does the same with his art. Robbe-Grillet claims that the new novel creates its own significations as it proceeds. This type of art refuses to answer the question: does reality have a meaning? The meaning of its reality is dependent upon the existence of the work itself; and meaning can only be spoken of after the work is completed. The *nouveau roman* in its construction resembles a labyrinth which is only recognized as being such when it is completed and all the roads are blocked and all the doors are shut. The whole world, as a result, is constantly being invented not only by artists but by all men, by all readers. Every man becomes a labyrinth maker. In dreams, memory, and insight, man's imagination is the organizing force which inexorably drives "things" out of their habitual categories and reinvents them in new maze-like structures: "Each man, in his turn, must reinvent the realities around him; these are the true, precise, hard and brilliant objects in the real world. They are not related to any other world. They are the sign of nothing other than themselves, and the only contact that man can have with them is through his imagination."[30]

In conclusion, because every character, novelist and reader reinvents the universe, the new novel aims at total subjectivity. Critics of the new form, however, claim that Robbe-Grillet's novels are too objective, too object-full. To this he responds that the narrators in his novels are far more engaged in the adventure than the omniscient narrator in Balzac's novels: "In my novels, for example, man is not only someone who describes everything, but he is the least neutral, the least impartial of men: he is *always* involved in a passionate adventure to the point of obsession, and often of deforming his vision and producing within himself imaginary states close to delirium."[31]

The foundation for the new novel, Robbe-Grillet sees clearly, is a new understanding of man—*"Nouveau roman, homme nouveau."* Man's situation in the world, he stresses, is not the same as it was a hundred years ago. As a result, the art he produces will mirror this. If the reader, then, has difficulty in his orientation in the modern novel, it is for the same reasons that man finds himself in a labyrinth where the old values and norms have disintegrated:

> And of course for the past twenty years things have been moving faster, although everyone recognizes that this is not the case with art alone. If the reader sometimes finds himself disoriented in the modern novel, it is in the same way that he sometimes feels lost in the very world he lives in, where the old establishments and laws are crumbling around him.[32]

Man has been accustomed to seeing himself as a center, as a master of the objects possessed by him. Now the order seems reversed. It is not man alone who defines the objects around him; they define him. What is at issue is reciprocal definition, not only because the significances around men are always partial, incomplete, tentative, and even contradictory, but because they are totally the product of his epistemology. Consequently, not only does the universe seem labyrinthine to man, but the universe reflects the fact that its author is himself a puzzle, a maze, and a labyrinth.

In Robbe-Grillet's cosmos, then, identity must be sought in the objects as they are distorted and reinvented by the seer-narrator. The novels reveal not only man's attempt to make sense out of the many labyrinths in which he makes his way, but that the labyrinths are in man himself. To be more precise, the labyrinth is man. He creates his self-labyrinth as he struggles to give significance to everything around him. In constant need of recovering his presence, every man is the labyrinth-maker, killing the monsters of the past, awaiting future cities.

### Dans le labyrinthe

Robbe-Grillet in *Dans le labyrinthe* uses the maze of the city and a soldier lost in it as the form of man's frustrations in his attempts at meaning. From the first paragraph of the novel to the end, the narrator contradicts himself almost as if the truth lies in neither of his statements. For instance, he opens with, "Outside it is raining, and you walk in the rain with head bowed, shielding your eyes with your hand."[33] At the end of the paragraph there is a parallel reversal, "Outside the sun is shining . . . and you walk in the bright sunlight, shielding your eyes with your hand" (p. 9). These contradictions are found right up to the end of the novel. Note for instance, the last paragraph of the novel: "Outside it is raining, and you walk in the rain with head bowed, shielding your eyes with your hand" (p. 219). This chiaroscuro technique, light, dark, sun, night, is strengthened by the description of the city with its parallel structure. The reader must also observe the importance of the I in both the light and the dark. In fact, after the opening sentence: "I am alone here, now, and well protected" (p. 9), the novel narrator does not again refer to himself until the very end when he says: "On *my* last visit, the third injection was useless" (p. 211), where the narrator seems to become the doctor in the novel. And again the personal pronoun is found in the very last sentence: "with the whole city behind me" (p. 221). It seems as if the whole quest in the novel of the labyrinth is this pursuit or journey for identity. The ambiguity in the narrator's identity, the mystery of the soldier and his box, seem to make the question of identity very important. The soldier seems lost in the city. Over and over again he meets the child from whom he tries to find directions. It seems as if the soldier is looking for pieces of thread as he tries to make his way through the city where he is a stranger and an alien. He seeks some kind of landmark or sign, but Ariadne's thread is now in broken fragments.

The novel's quest seems to demand the interpretation of the anonymous stranger: "In any case a street name would hardly furnish him with any useful information, in a city he did not know" (p. 31). Increasingly fatigued by his search, by the circles of light and the circles of darkness, the rows of streets and streetlights and apartment houses, the soldier finds himself in a pursuit conducted in a maze. Fatigue, alienation, and the meaninglessness of all his quests signify what it is to be in the labyrinth. The man appears in the labyrinth as a stranger and an alien, seeking clues to the meaning of the labyrinth. Instead, he finds clues only in the fleeting appearances of the child who does not know.

The story continues to trace the search of the soldier. He has been entrusted with this box by a dying soldier and has now made an appointment with someone to whom he will give the box. The box becomes a mysterious symbol and has been interpreted allegorically by critics, especially since the box is entrusted by the dying soldier to the narrator who will finally reveal the inconsequential contents of the box. Yet, the soldier even in his delirium never tires of trying to find the place:

> He did not know the city. He could easily miss the place. It was at the intersection of two perpendicular streets, near a street lamp. He had misunderstood or forgotten the names of the streets. He ignored the indications of maps, and did his best to follow the prescribed route. When he thought he was there, he waited. The intersection looked like the description he had been given, but the name did not resemble the vague sound he remembered. He waited a long time. He saw no one. (P. 208)

The soldier is constantly encountering crossroads as he waits for the someone to whom he must deliver the box. These crossroads become mysterious as he seeks the person who is to explain to him the meaning of his quest. Yet he finds nothing but the crossroads. He has wandered through the whole city and returned many times to the same place, but always in vain.

One of the most exciting aspects of the novel is the manner in which the novelist brings to life the contents of the painting *La Défaite de Reichenfels* and develops his story and his soldier out of his painting. Everywhere art in tension with reality and its characteristic constructs and structures, circles and parallel lines, mystify, bewilder, and beckon the protagonist, who is both the soldier and the reader, to try to find meaning. The narrator's last line, "with the whole city behind me," reinforces the interpretation of the novel as a quest through a maze of possibilities and crossroads and marks a frantic search for identity.

While the conflicts present in a person force him to be concerned about his true identity and real self, the weather and its contradictions mentioned by the narrator force the protagonist and reader to explicate the nature of the labyrinth. The labyrinth outside of man, outside of the protagonist, is described not only in its structure but also in its anonymity: "In any case, there are no tracks in the snow, no footsteps, and the snow, uniform, vertical and slow, continues to fall on the deserted street. The total blackness of night must now have fallen, for the flakes are no longer visible except when they pass the light of a street lamp" (pp. 77–78). There are no tracks in the snow and consequently no traces and no clues. Moreover, the patterns of dark and light follow one another so quickly that any trace of light is quickly blurred by the darkness. The labyrinth outside of man, outside the protagonist, finds its counterpart inside the protagonist. This doubling is achieved especially by the author's technique in maintaining the anonymity and obscurity of the narrator. The quest for identity, the absence of any personal pronoun in the narration except at the very beginning and the very end of the novel seem to reinforce the fact that the labyrinth, this quest for meaning, is also inside of man. Both structures, the structure of the city and the personal structure of the dying soldier giving the box to another soldier who dies, then to a narrator who seems to be at one time the soldier, at another the storyteller, and at another time the doctor emphasize a confusing search into the depths of personality and identity.

The whole quest of the labyrinth inside and the labyrinth outside is one in which the reader as well as the protagonist finds himself a stranger and an alien. He is a stranger in the city and also a stranger to himself. He has a mission to deliver a box. The mission may mean anything, but one thing is certain—it is fatiguing: "Once again he feels a great fatigue. He no longer wants to answer a questioning that leads to nothing. It wouldn't take much for him to hand over the box to a street urchin" (p. 45). The fatigue and the demands of the quest make him almost wish to abandon it. But he never does. He continues through the labyrinth and fulfills his mission. Dying, he gives the box to the "narrator" who reveals its contents, continues the story, and seems in the last line, "with the whole city behind *me*," to have left the labyrinth, found his identity, his "me." The story seems, therefore, to plot the journey out of the labyrinth as well. Although there are echoes and resonances of the whole quest in the last paragraph, the narrator has finally left the city behind him. The mission has been accomplished, the labyrinth has been conquered.

## *Le Voyeur*

Robbe-Grillet refuses to speak of his novels as "theory applied to art"; he prefers to define them in terms of exploration and invention. Invention, exploration, and discovery certainly form the narrative structure of *Le Voyeur*. As the title suggests, personality is found among the multiplicity of objects which result from the structuring powers of the one who sees. The tension between the different "seers" becomes clearer as the novel progresses. It is almost impossible at times to distinguish between what is peculiarly the vision of Mathias, the universe of Robbe-Grillet, the voyeur (Julien), and the projections of the reader.

Although this novel does not seem to be about labyrinths, the basic mythic archetype of the labyrinth is present. Since the eyes, the figure 8, and the infinity sign ∞ are all symbols for the labyrinth, each of these figures reinforces an interpretation which weaves together the labyrinths of reader, author, narrator, and characters. Interlocking labyrinths beckoning signification, inviting the murder of the monster and the revelation of its secret, tantalize the reader. Here, however, the thread of Ariadne can only be the reader's imagination.

The novel begins with a clear tension between the auditory and the visual. In spite of the shrill whistle of the boat, none of the passengers responded: "There was not a trace of movement on anyone's face ... It was as if no one had heard."[34] The faces of the passengers remained motionless to the sounds around them. Yet at the same time the reader is introduced to the "voyageur," Mathias, who is returning to the island of his birth as a salesman. He does not seem to hear, yet he *sees:* "he kept his eyes on the ground" (p. 9).

Some critics have identified the voyeur of the novel with the protagonist, Mathias. Others, like Bruce Morrissette, more wisely claim that the real voyeur in the story is the young Julien, who witnesses Mathias's act of murder. Although Julien may be the voyeur in the psychological sense of one who participates in evil simply by watching, the scope of the novel goes far beyond any one voyeur. Consequently, it would seem that Julien is simply one of many voyeurs among whom are Mathias, Robbe-Grillet, and particularly the reader.

The protagonist of the novel, Mathias, may be called an anonymous ''hero.'' And if the reader does not decide to give some meaning to the fantasies, memories, and hallucinations of Mathias, he remains an anonymous reader. The reader, in effect, is asked to create his own novel. In creating his own novel, the reader, Daedalus, becomes the prisoner of the labyrinths he himself creates. Yet, before this creation is possible, he must confront the tensions which the structure of the novel itself presents.

One of the more obvious characteristics of the narrative structure is the absence of the first person pronoun. Yet the third person narration does not indicate the author's point of view alone. Sometimes it does, as in the quote from the opening page: ''he kept his eyes on the ground'' (p. 9). Through this technique the author develops a type of cosmos or universe into which he inserts Mathias. This point of view or epistemological structuring seems to be the result of Robbe-Grillet's ''vision'' of the universe. Bruce Morrissette makes the following observation on this point: ''but in *Le Voyeur* it is the author himself, absent, impersonal but endowed with a special 'vision' of the universe of his own creation, who gives order to the world and the things in it, and then hands it over to his central character.''[35]

There are times, however, when Mathias' vision and Robbe-Grillet's seem at the point of union. It is Mathias and not Robbe-Grillet alone who projects the structure ''eight'' upon different objects. He sees a cord spread like an eight; birds fly in patterns of eights; and the imprint upon the shore seems to be in the form of an eight. The eight is not simply the structuring of the universe around Mathias, as Morrissette believes, but the result of Mathias's own projections. The reader learns later in the novel that this eight is a kind of symbol for the guilt which Mathias experiences after his crime. Robbe-Grillet prepares the reader for this by allowing Mathias to construct eight patterns early in the novel:

> Mathias tried to find a landmark. In a corner of the slip the water rose and fell . . .

> Against the rear vertical wall Mathias finally chose a mark shaped like an eight, etched clearly enough to serve as a landmark.[36]

Not only does Mathias structure many of his perceptions in patterns of eight, the reader finds himself doing the same thing as he observes Mathias ride across the countryside on a bicycle which is another example of two coupled circles. The use of the figure eight exemplifies the extent to which Mathias, Robbe-Grillet, and the reader all participate in the narration of the novel. Finally, in the constant reference to the eyes, again two coupled circles, the reader is forced to see the consistent structural base suggested by the title itself. In this structure, the eyes, the symbol eight (8), the sign for infinity ∞, and the labyrinth are all wedded. Each can stand for the other. The novelist provides labyrinthine material from which the reader makes his creation, his novel. The equality of symbols permits an overlapping of personae—creator and created, reader and character, character and author, the labyrinth and victims.

The high point of the phenomenon of seeing by *all* personae takes place in Julien's witness to Mathias's crime. Here again the reader is reminded that the psychological voyeur of the novel is Julien and not the criminal voyeur, Mathias: "Julien never took his eyes off the traveler, forcing him thus to speak, to speak rapidly, as rapidly as possible, but with the constant fear of losing what he said in wandering and trackless wastes" (p. 197).

Again and again Julien is described as one "with the same staring eyes" (p. 207). Mathias finally recognizes that Julien witnessed the murder of the girl: "Julien had 'seen.' There was no longer any point in denying it. The sights recorded by these eyes forever conferred on them an insupportable intensity" (p. 214).

Eventually, Mathias leaves the island without being accused of his crime. Here Robbe-Grillet's universe intrudes itself in geometric structures as the boat heads toward the mainland. It is at this point that the reader must confront the basic lack of overt moral and psychological articulation in the novel. In the first place, there is no retribution for Mathias's crime. Yet the more the novel refuses to consider the moral issue, the more is asked of the reader's own projections. R. M. Albérès observes this about the seeming lack of moralism: "The more the novel refuses to moralize, the more it bespeaks an implicit morality. Antimoralism, like the anti-novel and anti-literature, is an illusion, a contradiction in terms.''[37] Obviously the reader brings his own moral view and psychological status to a novel which seems to be devoid of this type of treatment. Is the reader's universe one in which evil or good is only gratuitously rewarded? If this is the case, Mathias simply is an example of this gratuity. On the other hand, if Mathias is psychologically ill or, in a word, schizophrenic, he is both tormentor and victim. The reader is again forced to realize that he has been duped, seduced, and identified with this fragmented individual as he tries to make sense out of his memories, hallucinations, and fantasies. Robbe-Grillet claims that the writer proposes and the reader disposes: the reader becomes God: ''If the reader has a moralizing mind, he will always find psychological and moral meaning. The writer doesn't forbid this, he invites it.''[38]

The interpretation of the novel rests ultimately with the reader. It is his preoccupations, biases, prejudices and imagination which define the novel as well as himself. In *Le Voyeur*, the persona of the reader is the point of view most sensitive to definition. It seems that he is the ultimate *Voyeur;* the one who sees, at the same time refrains and is compelled to judge and create. The realization that one is called to create a novel from the material which the writer suggests is both a challenge and a threat to the self who prefers ready-made significances.

While the whole novel allows the structuring power of the reader to construct his own novel, there is one scene which even permits the reader to see himself. Mathias returns to a café, and, while he is waiting to be served, he overhears a legend. The legend tells of a young girl who has to be sacrificed to a sea-monster while her sacrificer looks down on her and remains at the edge of the cliff. Although part of this story may be the result of Mathias's imagination, because of the crowd and his own headache, he seems to become two people at the same time. In fact, the sailor and the fisherman in the crowded café actually come between his two parts:

> Mathias finished his drink. He no longer felt the little bag between his feet, and looked down at the ground. The valise was gone. He put his hand into the pocket of his coat in order to wipe his greasy fingers on some bits of twine, all the while looking at the traveler. The waitress thought he was looking for money and shouted out the sum of his check; but he wanted to bargain over the price of the liqueur. So he turned towards the fat women, or towards the woman, or towards the girl, or towards the young waitress, then put down the valise in order to grasp the little bag

while the sailor and the fisherman mingled, intertwined, interposed themselves between the traveler and Mathias.

Mathias passed his hand over his forehead. It was almost night. He was seated on a chair in the middle of the street—in the middle of the road in front of the Black Rock café.

"Well, is that better?" asked a man near him dressed in a leather blouse.

"Yes, thank you, better," answered Mathias. He had already seen this man somewhere. He wanted to explain his discomfort and said, "It's the smoke, the noise, all these words . . ." He could say no more. But he got up without difficulty.[39]

Throughout the novel the protagonist is referred to as either Mathias or le voyageur. He is the stranger who returns to the island of his childhood to sell watches. In this passage the center of the person who calls himself Mathias becomes so detached from his function or role, that of voyageur, that the sailor and the fisherman can pass between. This is not only an amazing example of the criminal's fragmentation, it is also a sign of the possession of self-consciousness to such a distilled degree that the center can actually stand outside self.

The implications of a breakdown in identity are also present. The person becomes separated from the most profound sign of himself, his name (Mathias), and that which is his role or mask, voyageur. Since the reader has identified himself with both the role and the name of the protagonist, he undergoes the same experience. More than Mathias, who is not conscious of which part of him responds, the reader is reassured of identity in the answer to the gentleman's question: "Yes, thank you, better," answered Mathias. Mathias and not the voyageur, his role, responds. Mathias never again sees himself so objectified.

This incident allows the reader to question whether Julien, the viewer of the crime, is not a double or a mirror image of Mathias. Perhaps Julien is Mathias's creation or perhaps both of them create the reader; at times the reader feels like the witchdoctor in *Circular Ruins* of Borges who tries to dream and materialize a son only to find out that he himself has been dreamed by another. Even at the end of the novel, the reader still questions whether the murder of the girl is not merely the function of the imagination of Mathias as he projects himself into the legend he hears. On this level the reader gives significance to the universe of *Le Voyeur* and understands his own projections upon this universe. Although every novel is a composite creation of both writer and reader, much greater imaginative structuring is required of the reader of the *nouveau roman*. The reader becomes both dreamed and dreamer as he and the protagonist retreat into their own secret labyrinths and vanish together.

In conclusion, although the labyrinth myth is not explicitly referred to in *Le Voyeur*, the symbol is found in the structural base of the eye and the figure eight; the sign of the labyrinth mirrors the quest of the protagonist and the reader as they try to create meaning out of the maze of sense impressions. The murder of the girl becomes the monstrous center of the legend, and Daedalus becomes the reader.

The *nouveau roman* portrays an anonymous quest toward self-understanding through the metaphor of the labyrinth. New insight is the result of the journey; the new insight can be the metaphor for Athens, the city of wisdom, or it simply may mean that the person knows the labyrinthine city is behind. The connections between the labyrinth, the city, and the self are certain, but mysterious. In this respect, there is an amazing parallel between the last words of *Thésée* of Gide and the last sentence of *Dans le labyrinthe* of Robbe-Grillet. The narrator of *Thésée* says: "I left the city of Athens behind me."[40] The narrator of *Dans le labyrinthe* echoes this when he says: "The whole city behind me."[41] Being able to see the city behind one's shoulder means that the self has been victorious enough over the labyrinth to say with Thésée: "I have done my work for the good of future humanity. I have lived."[42]

# 6 / THE FICTIVE SELF AND IDENTITY

## LES FAUX-MONNAYEURS—ANDRÉ GIDE

Les Faux-Monnayeurs, which explicitly confronts the problems of authorial presence and identity in a novel, as a work of art has attracted divergent critical commentary. Some critics call it a novel chiefly of form.[1] Other critics prefer to see the novel as one in which the idea is more important.[2] The truth of the matter is that Les Faux-Monnayeurs superbly unites both form and idea to such an extent that the form itself confirms the problems which the content suggests. Carlos Lynes does not agree with this statement; he concludes his article on the form of Les Faux-Monnayeurs with a judgment that André Gide has failed: "This failure, moreover, strikes me as a failure to achieve a perfect solution to the problem of form, since it comes largely from the author's artistic procedure of refusing to 'follow through' either his characters or his story."[3]

This failure which Lynes alludes to is something which André Gide understood. In fact, he mentioned that some of the critics who condemn the novel will live to see it praised for the same vices which they find in it. It was during his trip to the Congo that he expressed this: "Within twenty years it will be acknowledged that the things originally censured in my book are precisely its best features. I am certain of it."[4] Furthermore, the reduction of the novel to form alone not only violates it as a work of art but seems to suggest a lack of awareness of the many dimensions in which Gide is writing. On the other hand, the reduction of the novel to a metaphysics destroys the art and fictive meaning of the work.

Through both its form and its content, *Les Faux-Monnayeurs* asks the reader to confront the problem of the author's fictive self and identity. All the problems which were discussed earlier, the problem of identity and isolation, the problem of identity in relationship to the other, the mask, the maze, are all present in both the form and the content of this novel. The novel seems to be made up of an infinity of mirrors. The plot centers around a novelist who is writing a novel which has the same title as André Gide's novel. Edouard, the novelist in *Les Faux-Monnayeurs*, keeps his journals in much the same way that André Gide composes his. The presence of the author in the work is admitted by Gide in his journals: "It is clear that this I, the novelist is the bearer in me of the character of Edouard; hence I must likewise bear within me the novel he writes."[5]

Both Edouard and André Gide constitute, create, doubles of themselves as they compose. Both are interested in mirrors and their reflections are prismatic. André Gide, in dedicating his work to Martin du Gard, cites him, quoting Thibaudet near the end of the *Journal des Faux-Monnayeurs* concerning the author's presence in the novel:

> It is rare that an author who reveals himself in a novel produces a character who resembles him, that is to say, a living individual ... The authentic novelist creates his characters with the infinite possibilities his life may hold; the false novelist creates them along the single line of his factual existence. The genius of the novel brings the possible to life; it is not simply a copy of the actual.[6]

This assertion of Gide is alluded to by Martin du Gard who claims, as Gide points out in the journals, that Gide only brings him in to prove him wrong: "Roger likes to play the role of the 'idiot' which I give him in 'If the Seed Does Not Die' ... and in *The Counterfeiters* I only bring him in to prove him wrong, I simply show him making some absurd objections, with the sole purpose of defending myself and showing that I am right to ignore him, etc.'"[7]

The experiences of André Gide and Edouard are also very much alike as their journals indicate. Demonstrating how different points of view experience reality, the novel shows how the truth is sought from a number of vantage points, all of them insufficient. Edouard in his journals claims that he is trying to write a novel in which the polarities between reality and the representation of it merge. This is, he claims, the deeper issue in his book.

> I am beginning to grasp what I might call the "deeper theme" of my book. It is, it will doubtless turn out to be rivalry between the real world and the way we represent it. The way in which the world of appearances imposes itself on us and in which we try to impose on the external world our particular interpretation is what constitutes the drama of our lives.[8]

The problem of reality, what it is, and the importance of the surface of something versus the depths of it are confirmed both by the form of the novel and by the content. Olivier, parodying Passavant who had stolen this from Paul Valéry, claims that "truth is appearance, mystery is form, and the deepest thing about a man is his skin."[9] Olivier's antagonism to the novel of ideas finds its clue in his defensiveness concerning Edouard who is writing a novel of ideas. For Passavant, Olivier's mentor, form is the all-important thing. For Edouard the idea is what is most important. Edouard is trying to write a novel in which depth is the entire issue. Passavant writes his with form as the guiding principle. André Gide in his novel manages to wed form and idea, Passavant and Edouard, into a perfect unity.

It is obvious that Gide is not of one mind with Edouard although he is very sympathetic. In Chapter VII of Part II, while the narrator reviews his characters, he claims that Edouard enrages him because he is sometimes the dupe of himself. Edouard, in his tremendous need for honesty and truthfulness in both his work and in his life, finds himself the very victim of what he wishes to avoid. While explaining his theory of the novel to Bernard, Sophroniska, and Laura, Edouard proposes that he is going to represent reality. His criticism of the naturalist school is that it is the representation of only one dimension of reality. He would like to put everything into his novel: " 'A slice of life,' said the naturalist school. The fault of this school was that it always cut its slice in the same direction: of time and length. Why not of breadth or depth? As for me, I would rather not cut it up at all. Understand what I say: I want to put everything into this novel.' "[10]

Lynes's reaction to this is that Edouard is rather naive in his attitude toward the novel. When Edouard tells Sophroniska that the title of his novel is *Les Faux-Monnayeurs* and that he is beginning with an idea, Bernard interrupts: "But why begin with an idea?"[11] Bernard then pulls out a ten franc counterfeit coin and shows how it sounds and rings exactly as a real coin, but when it is once worn down it is no longer counterfeit; it is simply what it really is, transparent glass. Edouard's reaction to this is that reality disturbs as well as interests him. Through his novel, Edouard is interested in what is deepest, not what is on the surface. He is not interested in the gold veneer but in the *glass* coin, off of which play the genuine colors of the personages in his intended novel. Edouard's idea of the novel and reality, however, is transcended by Gide's greater vision. The dispute between surface and depth is answered in the fiduciary value by which the person must live. Passavant and Edouard present a truth from a point of view which can only be transcended through trust. While allowing for betrayal, trust is the only possible exit from the demon which lies behind sincerity.

All the characters in *Les Faux-Monnayeurs* echo Gide's insistence on sincerity and truthfulness. In Edouard's first entry in his journals he shows how difficult it is to be sincere, since he feels that he is constantly changing:

> How irritating I find this question of sincerity! *Sincerity!* When I speak about it, I can only wonder about the sincerity of the word itself. If I come back to myself I can no longer understand what the word means. I am never anything but what I believe I am—and that is constantly changing so that often, if I were not on hand to introduce them, my being of this morning would not recognize that of this evening. Nothing can be more different from me than myself.[12]

The many phases and metamorphoses of the self seem to involve the deceptiveness of sincerity. Another section of the journals indicates how Edouard is obsessed with the problem of his own identity: "It doesn't seem to me that I have changed, precisely; but rather that only now am I beginning to be aware of myself. Up to this moment I didn't know who I was."[13]

Gide, the architect of Edouard and his novel, articulates Edouard's difficulty by relating it to the basic not-yet/becoming aspect of the person in his journals: "Nothing perhaps can be more damaging for certain men than the search for sincerity, which causes them to cast doubt upon some of their finest sentiments, and to think that they can be certain of nothing but the worst. I never am, I become. I become the one I believe (or you believe) I am.''[14]

André Gide suggests both in Edouard and in his own experience that a person *becomes* himself and that very often he becomes what he believes himself to be; if a person believes himself to be sincere or in love, he becomes sincere or in love. Gide realizes that a novelist who makes his hero struggle with self-knowledge is in a sense victimized by this obsession:

> If it is still a chimera at the age of twenty to think you know yourself well, it is positively dangerous at sixty to even look for such knowledge.
>
> My desire is no doubt sincere; but my desire to conquer it is no less so. This is not the important thing and may just lead me to calculations about the authenticity of the one or the other. The important thing is to know whether I am right in seeking to triumph over this desire, whether I am struggling from fear or virtue, from fear of others or of myself . . .
>
> The phrase that begins, ''I know myself . . .'' always ends negatively. ''I know myself: I do . . . not.''[15]

The heroes of the novel search for their identity, an identity which lies in the depths beneath the surface. Bernard intensely expresses this concern always to ring true, to be worth exactly what he appears to be worth: ''Oh, Laura! I should like, throughout my life, to give off, at the slightest touch, a pure, strong, authentic sound. Nearly all the people I have ever known ring false. That my worth should correspond exactly to what appears; not to try to appear more than what I am worth.''[16]

The need for sincerity and knowledge of oneself are very much bound up together. While Bernard wants to know himself and wishes to present himself as he really is, Edouard is doing the same in his preparation of his novel, and André Gide in an authorial, ''transcendent'' way is making the same attempts by pasting all the fragments of his characters together. This is another example of how the author is present in his characters' search for identity, for a self.

The novel as a whole relates the quest for sincerity. The problem of the journals bears this out. André Gide is present not only in his narrator who never allows the reader to forget that the work is fiction, he is present in his other personae, in the journals of Edouard, in the journals which he is keeping on *Les Faux-Monnayeurs,* and finally in the parallel journals of his whole life. Again and again the reader finds himself at the end of the gallery of mirrors. The most pronounced example of this is the instance in which Bernard is reading Edouard's journals and being filled in on the past. The fictive reality of Gide becomes Edouard's, who is watched by Bernard, whom the reader is watching. In all of them, in all of these mirrors that the reader sees, Bernard is watching Edouard and being watched. Another example of the importance of sincerity is revealed in the letter that Olivier sends to Bernard. It seems, as the narrator indicates, that the only sincere lines were those which were scratched out, that asked Bernard to tell his uncle, Edouard, that he misses him and loves him. The other parts of the letter were all lies.

The question, to what extent do letters and journals really present the truth, can be articulated in another way. To what extent does the writer mask himself in his journals, in his diaries, and in his letters? It is only the narrator who intrudes at this point and tells the reader that these last lines of Olivier had been scratched out and they were the only sincere ones in the letter. Again the novelist, Gide, never allows the reader to forget that he is reading fiction. His intrusion in a place like this allows for the fictive self of the writer to reveal himself for a moment and testify that sincerity totally embraced is only possible in fiction; that fiction, consequently, comes closer to the truth and depths of a person than more seemingly truthful writings. In the novel the author keeps the journals, the letters, and the fragmentary presentations of both plot and characters from becoming simply a multiplicity of tales. The form of the entire novel, consequently, not only confirms the ideas of the content but demonstrates a masterpiece of art. One of the ways in which this unity of form is achieved is through the ironic intrusion of the narrator's voice, parodying omniscience:

> The traveler arrives on the hilltop, sits down and takes a look before resuming his journey, which is getting tiresome. He tries to discern where he is going on this serpentine road which seems to him to be lost in shadow and, as evening is falling, the darkness of night. So too, the author takes care to stop a moment, catch his breath, and ask himself with some concern where it is his story will lead him.[17]

Never allowing the work to be seen as anything but fiction, the narrator manages to present the fictive selves of many points of view. As one of the central symbols of the novel, the gold piece, which is beneath its surface simply glass, has the same kind of force as the form does. The form of a novel, the appearance of a novel, pretends that it is something it is not, and as soon as the veneer or the surface is penetrated, it no longer can be called counterfeit reality, but fiction. Once the gold piece has its surface veneer removed it is no longer counterfeit. Stripped of its veneer the glass coin ironically becomes more valuable since it no longer can betray. Once fiction is preached as fiction it can never mask itself as counterfeit reality. The novel is exactly what it pretends to be, fiction. Gide manages in an extraordinary way to transcend pretentions at reality in fiction by a form which insists that once surfaces are scraped reality is no longer masked and counterfeited.

The peeling off of the mask through the form is found repeatedly through the novel in the peeling away of the characters' masks. Since their affections and poses are often merely pretense and counterfeit, their bonds are counterfeit bonds of affection. Once they are stripped of their masks, they are no longer counterfeit; they are, as the glass piece is, a transparent but authentic reality. Yet it is not so easy to strip personages, characters, and people of their surface masks, because the peeling off of one merely means the discovery of another.

Consequently, form again triumphs in portraying the meaning of the novel. While sincerity is so obsessively sought in self-identity and in motives, sincerity can often be the Achilles' heel of the character. The narrator candidly claims that it is the generosity of Edouard which makes him dangerous:

> What I don't like about Edouard is his reasoning. Why does he have to persuade himself that he is scheming for Boris's good? You can still get away with lying to others, but to yourself! Does the river that drowns a child pretend that it is giving him a drink? . . . I do not deny the existence in the world of noble, generous, and even disinterested actions; I am merely saying that behind the finest motivation there often lurks a clever devil who can make the best profit of what we thought we had taken away from him.[18]

It seems that even behind seemingly unselfish motives of generosity there lies a demon which betrays the generous person. Behind even the motive of sincerity, of truthfulness, of having things ring true, appear to be what they really are, there is also a devil. In wanting to have things always ring true, the demon of falsehood is present. Yet while André Gide constructs a new type of novel in *Les Faux-Monnayeurs* and never betrays the reader into thinking that it is reality he is experiencing and not fiction, he himself admits to his journals that the world of *Les Faux-Monnayeurs* is of the same stuff of reality as the exterior world—reminiscent of Borges's insights into the unreality of the real world: "It seems to me that we are all lurching around in a fantastic parade, and that what people call reality, their exterior world, no more exists than that of the *Counterfeiters* or the *Thibaults*."[19]

The promise of any novel is that its experiences are going to present a real world. The form's insistence on its fictiveness is ironically a commentary on all of reality. Moreover, the importance of the author's presence in the novel as well as his relationship to the form in which he works is found in the problem of persona. If persona is understood as a mask, the narrator can be, and often is, the fictive self of the author. This second self has been described as follows: "To put it in this way, however, is to understate the importance of the author's individuality. As he writes, he creates not simply an ideal, impersonal "man in general" but an implied version of "himself" that is different from the implied authors we meet in other men's works."[20]

In narrating the novel, the author's second self becomes the mask. Wayne Booth points out that, while the narrator, mask, and persona are sometimes used interchangeably, they are aspects of a wider technique which is the concretization of the author's own identity and many selves:

> It is a curious fact that we have no terms either for this creation "second self" or for our relationship with him. None of our terms for various aspects of the narrator is quite accurate. "Persona," "mask," and "narrator" are sometimes used but they more commonly refer to the speaker in the work who is after all only one of the elements created by the implied author and who may be separated from him by large ironies. "Narrator" is usually taken to mean the "I" of a work, but the "I" is seldom if ever identical with the implied image of the artist.[21]

In *Les Faux-Monnayeurs* the narrator is a persona or mask of Gide. Gide is trying to show how indispensable sincerity is even in fiction in his construction of the fictive self. Gide is larger than the narrator, since Gide's identity is partly found in the narrator but transcends him. This is evidenced in the ironic significance of the narrative structure. When the narrator intrudes, he seems to be telling the reader not to mistake this novel for reality. Gide goes beyond the narrator in expressing that the form and the content in fiction are an approach to reality. Gide is present in his work not only in the narrator but in his characters too, particularly his doubles, who are Bernard, Olivier, Edouard, and even Passavant. They indicate his presence as well as point to his absence. Their mirroring and prismatic function only finds its complement in the doubling quality found in musical counterpoint. In many ways the counterpoint of the novel's form as well as the reflections in the unmasked gold piece point out the many selves of the writer, Gide. In *Les Faux-Monnayeurs* he has given his readers a masterpiece of form and content. The form tells the same story that all his characters and the narrator create, a story which seduces man into believing that it is real, while all the time telling him that it is fiction. *Les Faux-Monnayeurs,* once stripped of its pretense, becomes like the glass piece of the story, mirroring all of Gide's masks and all his real and fictive experiences.[22]

The presence of the author in his work is difficult to pin down. In *Les Faux-Monnayeurs* readers are often tempted to identify Gide and Edouard. Yet the narrator prevents this total identification by his judgments on Edouard. The reader must also avoid identifying the narrator with the author Gide, since the narrator, too, is a character or a mask of Gide. An understanding of this is essential for confronting the problem of the author in his work and persona. Speakers and personae are easiest to observe in plays since the point of view changes each time a character does. This is not to be confused with the literary persona of the author, however, unless the character is the "raisonneur" of the playwright as Laudisi is of Pirandello. A treatment of persona in the poetry of Eliot, Yeats, and Pound has been developed by George T. Wright, *The Poet in the Poem*. Wright not only gives a history of the word and the function of persona but also relates the persona to self. His words on the technique of persona can also be applied to the novel.[23] While the author is hiding and revealing himself, he is also seeking and becoming himself, as Gide stated in his *Journal*. A very insightful statement about Gide's own presence and search in *Les Faux-Monnayeurs* has been made by Albert Guerard:

> Where Gide said that he is inhabited by the thoughts and feelings of others, he should have said that he projects his concerns into them, distributes his personality among them.

The great difference between *Les Faux-Monnayeurs* and the "récits" is not that it is less autobiographical in background, but that it is less subjective in tone.[24]

Gide's presence in this novel, then, finds its immediate mirror in the search and the masks of the characters. Through his personae the author is in his work; through his distinct personality as an artist he is beyond it. In this distinction lies the secret and mystery of every creator's identity—the secret of his Transcendence and his Immanence.

# 7 / LITERARY FORM AND PERSONAL IDENTITY

The obvious changes and innovations in literary form as well as in the contemporary understanding of the person suggest the possibilities of a relationship between the two. The issue is this: what do the changes in the identity of form, or genre, have to say concerning the meaning of personal identity and self? The fact that the novel, play, and poem all somehow indicate the disintegration of the character or hero raises the further question of how the character's identity relates to the disintegration and transformation of literary form. For instance, while Samuel Beckett and Robbe-Grillet in their innovations write novels that are very different from past novels as well as different from each other, they speak also of conscious changes in their own approach to the novel based on a new understanding of man. Robbe-Grillet, in his essay entitled ''Nouveau Roman, Homme Nouveau'' (1961), counters the objections that he is not writing a novel because he doesn't create characters, tell stories, or analyze passions, with the response that he is writing a *new* novel which is partially the result of a constant evolution:

> The error is to think that the ''genuine novel'' was determined once and for all in Balzac's time, according to strict and definitive rules. Not only has its evolution been considerable since the middle of the nineteenth century, but it began even in the time of Balzac himself. Is this not evident already in the ''confusion'' in the descriptions in *The Charterhouse of Parma*? It is certain that the battle of Waterloo as Stendhal describes it to us no longer belongs to the scheme of things set up by Balzac.[1]

Some critics like Eugene Goodheart in *The Cult of the Ego* see the changes in literary form, especially the new novel, as a cooperation with the destructive forces in life: "The new novel collaborates with what it presents in the sense that it offers neither judgment nor resistance."[2] For him the history of modern literature reveals a diminished control and resistance over the chaos of life. He cites Goethe's call for control over this chaos which should increase in proportion to emancipation and contends that this need for control is exactly what is not heeded by the new novelist.

Robbe-Grillet is particularly guilty in his judgment and Samuel Beckett whose characters with their "barbarously awkward syntax, the discontinuity of thought, the inept use of pronouns testify to the weariness with art as well as with life" (p. 198). Much contemporary literature, he insists, signifies a "conspiracy with the destructive tendency of modern life and 'teaches' us to accept it with almost perverse pleasure" (p. 4). All that is left, he writes, is perhaps no more than the artist's instinct for survival and that if it is not sufficient it may lead to the end of literature. Goodheart's thesis certainly should not be accepted without critical appraisal and perhaps a deeper confrontation with what Beckett, Robbe-Grillet, and other contemporary writers are all about. These two writers, while extraordinarily significant, neither in themselves indicate a decline in literature nor could they by themselves constitute that decline.

While the new novel also seems to be characterless to critics, Robbe-Grillet insists that it is interested in man and his situation in the world. In fact, "Man stands present on each page, at each line, in each word."[3] There is always implicitly present in a novel which is filled with objects, the seer or the viewer and his passion: "In our novels objects have no existence outside of the realm of human perceptions, real or imaginary; they compare to objects of our daily life, occupying our minds unceasingly."[4] Although man might seem absent midst the chaos of many objects and things, his unique type of presence is very much a reality and is determined by the form of the novel and the style which characterizes it. In fact, Robbe-Grillet insists that his novels are very subjective because not only is there a man who describes everything with great care, but because it is always the least impartial of men, someone who is always engaged in a most obsessive type of emotional adventure.[5] There is a very decided emphasis then on point of view in the new novel, a point of view which is very self-conscious and does not want to be mistaken for having any type of transcendent kind of knowledge of the event or the thing.

For instance, while Gide contributes his own transformations to the novel through the many points of view as they are presented in journals and letters, he also tries to unmask the idea that the author is omniscient. In a parody on the omniscient author, Gide concludes the second part of *Les Faux-Monnayeurs* with an author's judgment, so to speak, on his characters.[6] In the author's comments on his characters, he is adding another point of view, that of his *persona*. Although this is a departure from the "ordinary" novelistic point of view, Gide still portrays recognizable characters. The changes in form in a novel like *Les Faux-Monnayeurs* do not alter the image of man that greatly, since man and the person are described in recognizable terms.

Yet, the significance of the point of view of different narrators in determining the reality of character is a many-faceted problem. This is true not only in the works of French experimenters but of Americans as well. For instance, in Faulkner's *As I Lay Dying* the narrators' different perspectives determine the reader's interpretation of their characters. The narrator's character also determines the story which is pieced together by the novelist and, more accurately, by the reader whose interpretation and synthesis of the novel contribute to another creation. With the accumulation of points of view determining the character, the character becomes more important than the plot. If the reader wants to know how Darl differs from Cash in *As I Lay Dying*, all he has to do is compare the style of Darl's narration with that of Cash's. Or if he wants to know the difference between Cora's outlook on the world and Addie's, the words of their stories are the windows to their cosmos.

The story line, then, takes on significance only in terms of the character and how the character tells his story. For instance, in *The Sound and the Fury* of William Faulkner, the telling of the story four different times and in four different styles produces characters who are many-dimensional and prismatic. The opening paragraphs of each section alone say much about the narrators as characters. The nonintelligibility in Benjy's cosmos of relationship is illustrated by the first "incident" in which he mistakes the calling of a caddie for that of his sister's name. His inability to interpret events causally or chronologically illustrates his relationship to the world: "Then they went on, and I went along the fence. Luster came away from the flower tree and we went along the fence and they stopped and we stopped and I looked through the fence while Luster was hunting in the grass.'"[7] The style, which sounds very sequential here, also cannot really integrate memory data with that which is happening at the present. The style is one which concentrates on recording and not interpreting events. Because of this, the story becomes a description of Benjy. It is Benjy's story, and his view of the world creates it.

The second part of *The Sound and the Fury,* narrated by Quentin, immediately gives his construction of the world and at the same time defines him. Although it takes place in another time dimension, several years before the Benjy section, Quentin's obsessions with thought, guilt, and time tell the reader what his world is like through the style with which his story is created: "When the shadow of the sash appeared on the curtains it was between seven and eight o'clock and then I was in time again, hearing the watch. It was Grandfather's and when Father gave it to me he said, Quentin, I give you the mausoleum of all hope and desire.'"[8] Quentin's telling of the story is an addition to Benjy's, since it comes from another point of view. The Compson story becomes even more illusive and ends by being Quentin's story.

The third part, narrated by another brother, Jason, takes place on the day before the first section of the novel and reveals Jason's materialistic view of life as well as his hostility toward Quentin, Caddy, and Benjy. "Once a bitch always a bitch, what I say. I says you're lucky if her playing out of school is all that worries you.'"[9] Quentin gives his version of the story which shows how different his world is, and consequently his character, from Benjy's and Jason's. The final telling of the story is by a narrator who is not a member of the Compson family but a *persona* of Faulkner. The story takes place on the day after the first section of the novel. Here, even description shows a more distant point of view as well as the narrator's concern particularly with Dilsey as she somehow counteracts the sickness of the Compson vision. The narrator becomes, in a word, the author's *persona* and other self:

> The day dawned bleak and chill. A moving wall of grey light out of the northeast which, instead of dissolving into moisture, seemed to disintegrate into minute and venomous particles, like dust that, when Dilsey opened the door of the cabin and emerged, needled laterally into her flesh, precipitating not so much a moisture as a substance partaking of the thin, not quite congealed oil.[10]

The novel could continue in the telling of the story with many other

points of view from other members of the family as well as from out-
siders as in *As I Lay Dying*. The story, therefore, can constantly be
complemented by different characters in narration. The open-ended
story line is matched by the open-ended nature of personal definition.
However, what is significant here is that the plot is less important than
the character: man and personhood are emphatically at issue in this
kind of novel. Hardly absent, the person is the focal point of attention.
It is through his words, the mask of his personality, that the plot takes
shape.

Moreover, aspects of identity are brought out through theme and
symbol as well as through the technique of point of view. In Proust's
*A la recherche du temps perdu,* the form of the novel projects the same
meaning about the relationship of memory to personality and the self
that the experiences of Marcel, the protagonist, do. While Unamuno
may emphasize the continuity of personality which memory controls,
Proust's narrator has to overcome the pitfall of voluntary memory
which can sometimes deceptively structure experiences into cause and
effect. It is only in the numerous episodes in which involuntary or
affective memory takes over that aspects of self are recovered. Here
the person preserves a continuity of personality over the fragments
of experiences through the surfacing effect of involuntary memory. An
example is Marcel's unbuttoning of his boots several years after his
grandmother's death bringing back to him not only the felt presence
of his grandmother and the reality of her death but an aspect of himself
that had been lost to him. There are many other examples of this type
of rediscovery in the novel, including the famous instance of the
*madeleine* dipped in the tea. At moments in which this experience takes
place, Marcel rebecomes himself. Proust's narration and the individual
episodes illustrate the point that the entire self does not exist all at
once. The person has to overcome the many fragments of self which
the cloudiness of memory has covered in order to find himself through
the intermittences of the heart.

Unfortunately, voluntary memory sometimes reveals a lost and dis-
oriented "I" because of the changes in events and places. The end of
*Du côté de chez Swann* manifests a disappointed Marcel, hopelessly
trying to evoke a moment that could not be recalled because Mme.
Swann's nonappearance changed the whole avenue and the self's relationship to it. Through both the form of the novel and the episodes,
Marcel's personality unfolds, overcoming the fractures of self through
affective memory. The unfolding and the episodes corroborate the

search for self and emphasize the way man now sees himself. It is no longer through the logical and chronological telling of one's life that the person comes to be, forming the usual expression of plot. Here the plot of the realistic novel would only betray Proust's fundamental truth about the self; that is, that it does not exist all at once, but is recoverable only in isolated moments of involuntary recollection:

> At whatever moment we estimate it, the total nature of our spiritual nature is more or less fictitious, notwithstanding the long inventory of its treasures, for now one, now another of these is unrealisable . . . Now, inasmuch as the self that I had just suddenly become once again had not existed since that evening long ago when my grandmother undressed me after my arrival at Balbec, it was quite naturally, not at the end of the day that had just passed, of which that self knew nothing, but—as though there were in time different and parallel series—without loss of continuity, immediately after the first evening at Balbec long ago, that I clung to the minute in which my grandmother had leaned over me.[11]

Marcel, then, "recreates" himself through a unique type of structuring in time.[12] The importance of structuring and recreating is emphasized in today's literature also as the necessary work of the reader. While this has always been the role of the reader, his structuring and creative ability seem to be singularly important in the cosmos of Beckett and Robbe-Grillet. Sartre claims the error of realism was to believe that the real reveals itself to contemplation.[13] If all the author does is reveal, and the reader merely absorbs, the reader's right to creativity is neglected; a creativity which means he is bringing himself to the interpretation of the work to such an extent that his interpretation means self-creation. This is as much true in Kafka as in Robbe-Grillet, he insists. For, as Sartre points out, the boundaries of realism and truth in Kafka's mythology are never given. He claims the reader must invent the meaning in a continual exceeding of the written word: "To be sure, the author guides him, but all he does is guide him. The landmarks he sets up are separated by the void. The reader must unite them; he must go beyond them. In short, reading is directed creation."[14] The reader's identity then is inextricably wed to the change of form, as Robbe-Grillet insists, through the changing identity of man himself.

Man, however, must survive the metamorphosis. Gregor, in Kafka's

*Metamorphosis,* is an example of nonsurvival. Edwin Honig insightfully expresses the reason for Gregor's lack of survival:

> Since he cannot assert any actual sense of himself, he falls prey to those forces in himself and in others that have hopelessly mistaken him. It is as if he negatively and inevitably "self-awares" himself out of existence on learning how arbitrary his identity is; or how, in depending so largely on others, it must perish for lack of the right sustenance.[15]

Totally alienated, Gregor gradually disintegrates in his dialogue with the "normalcy" of the unreal reality that he wakes into. The chasm between the worlds of Gregor and the Samsas overwhelms him. One reading of the story could see Gregor as dead at the beginning of the story because of his inability to cope with himself and his relationship to the world. His change is a concretization of a reality that is already present in him during his "unquiet dreams." Guilt, loneliness, impotency are the tensions which conflict in the ego's survival over annihilation. Kafka, Camus, Proust, Joyce, Robbe-Grillet present in different forms man's need to survive—in a world which more and more challenges man to be a self-creative person, fashioning himself honorably in his struggle to exist.

This struggle to survive may be depicted today in terms of a consciousness projected onto things as in Robbe-Grillet, or it may arise in the telling of the story in order to construct meaning out of the events in one's life as in John Hawkes's *Second Skin.* The cause-effect sequence, a large part of a former way of finding identity in the cosmos, has been replaced by the nonlogical sequence, present in an examination of conscious as well as subconscious activity. For instance, through an examination of the interiority of a character's memory and through interior monologue, Proust reveals how difficult it is for a person to find a consistent personality in the reconstruction of events. Skipper, another "fictive autobiographer" in Hawkes's *Second Skin,* survives in two ways: as a human being in as much as he doesn't fall victim to the self-destruction of suicide like his father and daughter, and as a storyteller who explores the events in his life for meaning. Skipper's story is like a dream remembered. Here memory links the dreamer to his life. The telling of the dream like the dream itself has its own kind of logic and represents a triumph over chaos. Skipper is both naive and sophisticated in his approach to events. His naiveté confronts the reader as he begins by "naming names," which introduces the reader to the personages of his tale, and performs what Sartre calls a revelation of the inessential. Yet the telling of his life and the reconstruction of events give evidence of a sophistication and wisdom through an implicit knowledge that the meaning of the events in his life do not necessarily depend upon a causal, logical, and chronological sequence. A would-be poet, he distorts reality, in order to survive, into a continual victory over his memories and the people in his life like Miranda and Cassandra. This is evidenced in his approach to nature through his language whose lyricism, conflicting at times with the tragic events of his life, gives his story a macabre beauty. Yet Skipper's story, even in its parodic moments, for him means survival. Names are seen as no longer really important to him at the end, as he sees the outline of the stone in the cemetery with no name and no date, yet *surviving* grief without any real need to be identified by words.

While *Second Skin* narrates Skipper's survival and at times seems to be a parody of it, *Under the Volcano* by Malcolm Lowry depicts a man who does not survive and who never manages to write his life-book. Lowry's protagonist, the Consul, because of his inability to give meaning to his life does not survive. This novel may be a helpful complement to the antirealistic novels as an illustration that the same type of quest goes on through a more traditional form.

While the story of the Consul is told logically and chronologically, as opposed to the nonlogical sequence of the *nouveau roman*, the psychological realism of the story manifests the conflicts in the inner man. Firmin has to struggle against the haunting loneliness and guilt which drive him to drink, which continually try to rob him of himself, and which, ironically, he does not want to give up.

> When he had striven upwards, as at the beginning with Yvonne, had not the "features" of life seemed to grow more clear, more animated, friends and enemies more identifiable, special problems, scenes, and with them the sense of his own reality, more *separate* from himself? And had it not turned out that the further down he sank, the more those features had tended to dissemble, to cloy and clutter, to become finally little better than ghastly caricatures of his dissimulating inner and outer self, or of his struggle, if struggle there were still?[16]

The novel religiously describes Firmin's temptation to self-annihilation and his struggle to survive. He is not alone, however, in confronting the burden of loneliness, anxiety, and guilt. His half-brother, Hugh, and his wife, Yvonne, face the same threats. The novel magnificently —through realism and symbol—shows how they all strive to cope with the forces which war on self. For instance, in a wedding of realistic description to symbol, Yvonne and Geoffrey look for each other and just miss each other in the restaurants and bars the night before she leaves Geoffrey. This is just one of the many experiences of unattainable union and wholeness needed to triumph over the isolation that destroys self. All the characters are encircled by the threat of death and war, realistically described and symbolically suggested.

The relationship between exchanges of roles and identity is brought out in the scene in which the group meets the dying Indian on the road and in the last scene. Firmin becomes both the dying Indian, the outcast, and the people who steal his money. The proximity of death, the pervasive loneliness, anxiety, guilt, and the exchange of roles not only construct a brotherhood of fellow sufferers but present myriad reflections of each person's struggle to survive.

This novel, then, pursues the theme realistically in its descriptions, and symbolically in the chronological passing of one day which represents a whole lifetime. Refrains like "a corpse will be transported by express" and "the Pope's death is inevitable," references to the war in Spain and to the descriptions of the dying Indian project a powerful symbolic metaphor for the all-pervasive cloud of death. Thoughts of Judas, the guilt in the theme of the Peter Lorre film, Yvonne's anxiety over her rejection, and the betrayal on Hugh's part present the guilt that all the central characters have to confront. Finally the symbol of the Pariah dog, the image of the outcast following Firmin through town and eventually into the ravine makes the Faustian Consul a compellingly sympathetic character who is unable to give up his aloneness to survive. Unfortunately, Firmin sees his identity in terms of an outcast, and to give that up means ironically to lose himself.

While the plot of this novel and the characters and description are realistic, the many symbols which link all of them show man's desperate attempts to survive in a new type of world: "My battle for the survival of the human consciousness" expresses the Consul's struggle against the annihilation that eventually befalls him. Malcolm Lowry, like Joyce, portrays this attempt to preserve self and identity chiefly through psychological realism. This same tension between existence presence. Regardless of how intense the search for person is in Pirandello, the characters are always "life-like," they are there on the stage, they are to be recognizable people in their quest. In fact, Pirandello insists that the "personaggi" should appear more real than his real characters. They are no longer the symbolic representations of disintegrated persons that syntax alone can proclaim. Here their disintegration must be represented by something other, perhaps by the ragged dress of a vagabond or a tramp as in *Waiting for Godot* or by the period-costume of *Enrico IV* of Pirandello.

While being a character in a play, as Robbe-Grillet suggests, means to be there, the most significant kind of absence on the stage is that in which the character is talked about but never manages to appear. Here the significance of Godot takes on a new dimension. He is not only the sought after experience of Gogo and Didi, but he is himself someone who never manages to be on the stage, to acquire a personality, to be "there" in terms of a dramatic character: "And so all these creatures that have passed before our eyes have merely tricked us; they are like those words in a novel which replace the indefinable being that never comes into view, the man incapable of achieving his own existence, the one who never manages to be present."[24] Godot is he who never is allowed the reality of a stage character. From the speech of the boy who appears as Godot's messenger, the audience knows that he has two servants, one who minds the goats and the other who minds the sheep. But Godot himself, while remaining a character, never manages to be a "stage" character.

While character or personhood on the stage differs from character in the novel, both show the preoccupation with the search for the self, for the reality of the person. This is evidenced particularly in the anguished cries of the "personaggi" of Pirandello as they try to decipher the distance between their mask, the masks of others, and their real selves. The stage is a perfect setting, then, for the characters' reduction through a particular type of stage absence. The vestigial self of the stage character comes across not only in the unique fashion of Godot's nonappearance, but also in the abrupt, abbreviated, nonlogical dialogue that takes place. This dialogue, which can take the form of parody and humor, reinforces the lack of real or complete personhood that the character represents. Even on stage, characters are not whole. In *Endgame* Hamm and Clov are incomplete; Hamm who is blind cannot stand up. Clov cannot sit down. Each needs the other for completeness; yet their dialogue, even when put together, remains somehow incomplete. For instance, this dialogue exchange which seems to pass the time is an attempt at communication but more exactly a parody of it:

> CLOV: He's got away.
> HAMM: He can't go far. (*Pause. Anxious.*) Eh?
> CLOV: He doesn't need to go far. (*Pause.*)
> HAMM: Is it not time for my pain-killer?
> CLOV: Yes.
> HAMM: Ah! At last! Give it to me! Quick! (*Pause.*)
> CLOV: There's no more pain-killer. (*Pause.*)
> HAMM: (*appalled*): Good ... ! (*Pause.*) No more pain-killer!
> CLOV: No more pain-killer. You'll never get any more pain-killer. (*Pause.*)
> HAMM: But the little round box. It was full!
> CLOV: Yes. But now it's empty. (*Pause. Clov starts to move about the room. He is looking for a place to put down the alarm-clock.*)
> HAMM: (*soft*): What'll I do?[25]

This verbal interchange illustrates the vacuity of their life together as well as the incompleteness of their self. The disintegrated syntax of *How It Is* becomes in a play the broken non sequiturs of dialogue.

Hermann Hesse in an interview with Miguel Serrano claims that language is like a veil:

> "Words are really a mask," he said. "They rarely express the true meaning; in fact they tend to hide it. If you can live in fantasy, then you don't need religion, since with fantasy you can understand that after death, man is reincorporated in the Universe."[26]

The problem of words being a mask and becoming themselves a personality is very much present in the new writers' approach to language. The words are not only a means for communication, they become the form itself. Perhaps the words are not only mimicking the commonplace, trite, and empty language of our daily expression, but they are also unmasking its vacuity and hypnotizing the reader with a pseudo-personality. For the words themselves take on a personality, whether they are the words of Gide in *Les Faux-Monnayeurs* the words of the narrator of *How It Is*.

and extinction is presented differently in the *nouveau roman,* whose technique utilizes the metamorphosed man still searching for a presence.

*Pale Fire* by Vladimir Nabokov does not belong to either the psychological realistic school or to the *nouveau roman,* yet it is another example of the changing genre of the novel and its relationship to identity. It consists of a foreword and a commentary by Kinbote on a poem by John Shade, his friend. The humor in the novel, as has often been noticed, is the result of the difference between the farfetched commentary's literary apparatus and the poem by Shade. In Kinbote, Vladimir Nabokov constructs not only a comic character but one who in the act of creating possesses a pride which encompasses an enormous lack of self-knowledge. Kinbote's mistake is not simply one of methodology, then, but of a lack of self-recognition. He becomes an ironic character whom the reader understands because of the sympathetic yet often homiletic smile of the transcendent author, Nabokov. Kinbote's attempt at scholarship is fused with his need to seem friendly and convince the reader of his worthiness to be a friend. His ''erudition'' is interrupted not only by inconsistencies, digressions, and irrelevancies but even by attempts to be familiar with the reader as in ''Canto Two, your favorite.'' In spite of the fact that he is parodied as haughty by the drama students, Kinbote really wants to be liked and respected; for he reminds the reader that even perceptive people like the Shades befriend and confide in him. This is what gives him such a superior position in relationship to Shade's poem. Kinbote's pretension as a creator and his pride, while causing much of the humor in the novel, also illustrate a truth about creating in general. Kinbote completely misses the mystery involved in creating. His error is to make static and infallible what should remain open and subject to new meanings and discoveries. Literary apparatus should suggest to the reader possibilities for his own imaginative creating. Thus every act of creation and structuring means that the creator must allow for his work to be seen as somehow unfinished, waiting to be completed by what another person can bring to it. This is hardly the attitude of Kinbote evidenced by the following advice: ''the reader is advised to consult them [the notes] first and then study the poem with their help, rereading them of course as he goes through its text, and perhaps after having done with the poem, consulting them a third time so as to complete the picture.''[17]

Kinbote's pride gives him the position of a god who has the definitive word. Nabokov through the foreword and apparatus, creations of Kinbote, expands the figure of Kinbote as does Joyce in Bloom and the citizen in the Cyclop's section of Ulysses through a type of gigantism. This gigantism is also complemented by deflation. For in his pride and inability to laugh at himself, Kinbote forces the reader to laugh at him. Yet he remains a sympathetic character, perhaps because the reader knows him so well, sees him as a solitary figure who needs to be befriended and respected and most of all as a figure who *fails*. For with all of the apparatus Kinbote doesn't seem to understand the parodic nature of Shade's poem. Nabokov allows the reader a privileged place by his side; like gods on a mountain-top, Nabokov and his readers look down on Shade and Kinbote, smile at their creations and at each other, and discover that there is an immense part of themselves in Shade and Kinbote, their fictions. In his translations and notes on Pushkin's *Eugene Onegin,* Nabokov realizes a type of scholarship that his pretentious Kinbote could only parody. In a sense, Kinbote is the opposite of Edouard of *Les Faux-Monnayeurs.* For, while both are writers or creators, Edouard is obsessed with the need for self-knowledge as he writes and Kinbote by a decisive absence of it. While the Consul of Lowry is driven to self-annihilation, and Shade survives only beyond the commentary, Kinbote is the invincible clown with many faces: "I shall continue to exist. I may assume other disguises, other forms, but I shall try to exist."[18] In a sense Shade and Kinbote survive in each other as polarities of a more encompassing self; the madman or clown is the poet's other face. As the moon is an arrant thief snatching her pale fire from the sun, Kinbote depends on Shade. Yet their light comes from the same source, an energy common to both of them, found only in their creator's transcendent circumference. If Kinbote in some way represents the clown in Shade and Nabokov, he also mirrors the truth that modern man must see the clown in himself to survive. Kinbote, of course, cannot. He would be a reluctant member of the community of vagabonds that Beckett reveals to us or of the sophisticated, yet ironic, maze-makers of Gide and Borges. Nabokov provides a valuable service in the fact that he permits us to see that in all of us one of our selves is a clown whom we do not recognize as we take overseriously the problems of our paths to self.

While character, then, seems very important to Gide, Faulkner, Lowry, and Nabokov, at first glance the novels of Robbe-Grillet seem to suggest that characters are not important to him, that neither character nor plot is essential. Certainly the change and transformations in the form of his novel reflect a change in understanding of the person.

While Faulkner's transformations and innovations in the novel, for instance, allow the person to be the focal point of attention through narration and point of view, Robbe-Grillet's description of objects and things creates a precarious presence for a person. He insists that objects suggest point of view. In *La Jalousie,* for instance, the narrator tells the place of the chairs because the description itself reflects and intensifies the tensions within the narrator and his preoccupation with his wife's feelings toward his friend, Franck:

> And so she had Franck's chair on her left, and on her right—but moved forward—the little table with the bottles on it. The other two chairs were placed on the other side of this table, still further to the right, so as not to interfere with the view between the first two and the balustrade of the terrace. With the same concern for the "view," these last two chairs were turned away from the rest of the group.[19]

The obsessions with the stain on the wall in *La Jalousie* and the number of times it is described, even though the plot is very simple, forces the passion of the narrator to become clearer and clearer. His jealousy is constantly evoked by the things and objects themselves. The reader might conclude that the narrator is simply a caricature of the jealous person since he does not know too much about any other of his characteristics except this one dominating passion and obsession. The reader does know enough about the character, however, to see that it is passion which determines the story.

In the novels of Samuel Beckett there is an evolution which is displayed not only in the disintegration of the character or hero, but by a more disintegrated syntax as well. Compare, for instance, the type of narration in *Murphy* to that in *The Unnamable.*

> The sun shone having no alternative, on the nothing new. Murphy sat out of it, as though he were free, in a mew in West Brompton.[20]
>
> Where now? Who now? When now? Unquestioning. I, say I. Unbelieving. Questions, hypotheses, call them that. Keep going, going on, call that going, call that on.[21]

The I of *The Unnamable* is simply a voice who is asserting his existence among a multiplicity of questions and words. His style, his way of expressing himself, is different from the narrator's telling of Murphy's story. Murphy, however, is a more fully drawn character, while the Unnamable is merely a vestige of self. The self becomes even more vestigial in *How It Is*. Here, not only has the syntax disintegrated, but the form in which the words appear has disintegrated as well; they are not long blocks but verse-like:

> how it was I quote before Pim with Pim after Pim how it is three parts I say it as I hear it voice once without quaqua on all sides then in me when the panting stops tell me again finish telling me invocation

> past moments old dreams back again or fresh like those that pass or things things always and memories I say them as I hear them murmur them in the mud.[22]

The way the words fall onto the page suggests words articulated in between gasps for breath as the I or the self continues. The words flow in hypnotic relationship to one another and almost take on a personality of their own. Here the form adequately expresses the changing understanding of man. Robbe-Grillet's insistence that the new novel reflects man's changed understanding of himself seems quite accurate. The significance of the new novel is dependent upon meaning which the reader gives it, for the novel itself is the result of different narrators creating a plot that can never be complete since the points of view are ever open. Even if the cosmos is that of an object-full chaos marked by a disintegrated syntax, the person of the narrator is present in his own story, in the objects which he describes so carefully, in his reasons for doing so, in his words as well as in the spaces.

A character in a play differs fundamentally from a character in a novel. Speaking of Samuel Beckett, Robbe-Grillet claims, "the theatrical character is on the stage, that is his primary quality: he is there."[23] While a voice alone can exist in a novel, and the shred of personhood through his voice or disintegrated syntax, the character in a play usually has to maintain some type of presence on a stage for him to be understood as a character, for him to be there. If there were just a set without any characters the audience would have to project their own characters or their own meaning into the set. This is the context in which the new play differs from the new novel. It is not the characters' or the narrator's description of objects in a play which is important, but his presence on the stage and more importantly the *signs* of his presence. Regardless of how intense the search for person is in Pirandello, the characters are always "life-like," they are there on the stage, they are to be recognizable people in their quest. In fact, Pirandello insists that the "personaggi" should appear more real than his real characters. They are no longer the symbolic representations of disintegrated persons that syntax alone can proclaim. Here their disintegration must be represented by something other, perhaps by the ragged dress of a vagabond or a tramp as in *Waiting for Godot* or by the period-costume of *Enrico IV* of Pirandello.

While being a character in a play, as Robbe-Grillet suggests, means to be there, the most significant kind of absence on the stage is that in which the character is talked about but never manages to appear. Here the significance of Godot takes on a new dimension. He is not only the sought after experience of Gogo and Didi, but he is himself someone who never manages to be on the stage, to acquire a personality, to be "there" in terms of a dramatic character: "And so all these creatures that have passed before our eyes have merely tricked us; they are like those words in a novel which replace the indefinable being that never comes into view, the man incapable of achieving his own existence, the one who never manages to be present."[24] Godot is he who never is allowed the reality of a stage character. From the speech of the boy who appears as Godot's messenger, the audience knows that he has two servants, one who minds the goats and the other who minds the sheep. But Godot himself, while remaining a character, never manages to be a "stage" character.

While character or personhood on the stage differs from character in the novel, both show the preoccupation with the search for the self, for the reality of the person. This is evidenced particularly in the anguished cries of the "personaggi" of Pirandello as they try to decipher the distance between their mask, the masks of others, and their real selves. The stage is a perfect setting, then, for the characters' reduction through a particular type of stage absence. The vestigial self of the stage character comes across not only in the unique fashion of Godot's nonappearance, but also in the abrupt, abbreviated, nonlogical dialogue that takes place. This dialogue, which can take the form of parody and humor, reinforces the lack of real or complete personhood that the character represents. Even on stage, characters are not whole. In *Endgame* Hamm and Clov are incomplete; Hamm who is blind cannot stand up. Clov cannot sit down. Each needs the other for completeness; yet their dialogue, even when put together, remains somehow incomplete. For instance, this dialogue exchange which seems to pass the time is an attempt at communication but more exactly a parody of it:

> CLOV: He's got away.
> HAMM: He can't go far. (*Pause. Anxious.*) Eh?
> CLOV: He doesn't need to go far. (*Pause.*)
> HAMM: Is it not time for my pain-killer?
> CLOV: Yes.
> HAMM: Ah! At last! Give it to me! Quick! (*Pause.*)
> CLOV: There's no more pain-killer. (*Pause.*)
> HAMM: (*appalled*): Good ... ! (*Pause.*) No more pain-killer!
> CLOV: No more pain-killer. You'll never get any more pain-killer. (*Pause.*)
> HAMM: But the little round box. It was full!
> CLOV: Yes. But now it's empty. (*Pause. Clov starts to move about the room. He is looking for a place to put down the alarm-clock.*)
> HAMM: (*soft*): What'll I do?[25]

This verbal interchange illustrates the vacuity of their life together as well as the incompleteness of their self. The disintegrated syntax of *How It Is* becomes in a play the broken non sequiturs of dialogue.

Hermann Hesse in an interview with Miguel Serrano claims that language is like a veil:

> "Words are really a mask," he said. "They rarely express the true meaning; in fact they tend to hide it. If you can live in fantasy, then you don't need religion, since with fantasy you can understand that after death, man is reincorporated in the Universe."[26]

The problem of words being a mask and becoming themselves a personality is very much present in the new writers' approach to language. The words are not only a means for communication, they become the form itself. Perhaps the words are not only mimicking the commonplace, trite, and empty language of our daily expression, but they are also unmasking its vacuity and hypnotizing the reader with a pseudo-personality. For the words themselves take on a personality, whether they are the words of Gide in *Les Faux-Monnayeurs* the words of the narrator of *How It Is*.

## Literary Form and Personal Identity

Through his words the character is drawn. Not only do these words form a point of view and indicate an epistemology, but they also seem to become a mask and take on a personality. This is particularly true in the poetic style or form of dialogue exchange between Gogo and Didi, or in the hypnotic expression of *The Unnamable* or *How It Is*. Words themselves mask personality and become themselves a particular type of persona. The flow of words, whether they appear in dialogue or in the monologue of the Unnamable's unending verbal quest, almost takes the shape of a character. It seems, therefore, that the changes and transformations of genre are definite signs of changes in the understanding of man. The words themselves are forced into significance by the reader. They cannot be merely the one-dimensional significance of any one person, for the author's intention is to show that man's words —language and literary form—reflect the change in the nature of man's identity. As Robbe-Grillet insists, the evolution of man demands changes in literary form. In a word, these changes in literary form mirror a changing man, struggling in a world that often seems to want to rob him of his presence.[27]

# CONCLUSION

In the search for identity this study has explored the following dimensions of personhood: the relationship of the consciousness of an individual to self, the witness of the other in defining the self, language, masks and self, the labyrinthine patterns within and outside the self, and finally creativity and the self. In all these different avenues of exploration one of the most central aspects is the creativity of the searcher. The definition of self seems constantly open to new discoveries which only partially exhaust a definition. In these discoveries, whether they be aspects of witness or of consciousness or of the mask, the person is most himself when he creates. The creator, then, is most essentially the ground of person and personality.

To be a person means to some extent to be not finished, not yet, not yet defined, and not yet ready for definition.[1] Identity means more than exploration; it means self-invention. Perhaps the most significant *desideratum* of an identity quest is that which comes about through the possibilities which creativity reveals. Creativity meaningfully links together the various areas of self-exploration. A very significant confirmation of the previous exploration is found in the insights revealed in the creation stories. The synthetic aspects of the search are brought together in a richly meaningful way in the creation account in the Book of Genesis as well as in the prologue of St. John. The prologue takes a pre-existent Christian hymn and highlights the essential tensions and themes of John's Gospel. It echoes the creation account of Genesis and introduces the reader of the gospel to the person of Jesus of Nazareth through a hymn to the Word.

# Conclusion

Because of the synthetic aspects of this prologue, this conclusion will link the different aspects of the search for person and identity through a parallel in the creation account of John in the hymn to the Word. In this hymn the witness of the other, consciousness, labyrinth, mask, and creation are all related to the different elements of the search already explored. The conclusion, then, will treat synthetically what has already been the subject of analysis.

Moreover, while the prologue is an introduction to the person of Jesus of Nazareth, its mythical energy contains a profound statement on the meaning of selfhood. The hymn begins with the relationship of the Word with God, the Creator: "In principio erat Verbum, et Verbum erat apud Deum, et Deus erat Verbum" (John 1:1). The relation between the Word, the Logos, and God is not only seen in the preposition *apud,* which, according to Mollat's exegesis signifies the presence of the Word with God and also indicates a personal relationship with God, the Creator.[2] The Word is identified with God: "et Deus erat Verbum." This identification is one in which both consciousness and the expressed or uttered word are important. In the study of *Monsieur Teste* and *Murphy,* the attempt at identity or at reaching the self is made in terms of self-consciousness, with the exclusion of the otherness of people or even at times of one's own body. The relationship of the Word with God is through a consciousness which pre-existed even the otherness of creation. God's identity is founded in His consciousness of Himself with the Word as John says, "In Principio," in the beginning, before creation. The significance of consciousness in determining the self or identity is that of necessity, since without consciousness the Word, the Logos, could not exist as the conscious expression of the Creator. Bernard Lonergan's explanation of the procession in the Trinity is one based on an intelligible emanation which is founded in a conscious act: "Thus an intelligible emanation is the conscious origin of an act both within the intellectual consciousness and in virtue of that very intellectual consciousness actually determined."[3] The relationship of the Word, the Logos, to the Theos is based on a relationship of one conscious act arising from another. This conscious act relationship is analogous to the conscious finite act in man, according to Lonergan. In God, however, this conscious act is infinite: "And so by one act the infinite God looks at his own infinite perfection and intellect; he makes an act of affirmation in virtue of the perfection he sees, and he loves in virtue of the perfection he affirms."[4] The Verbum, or Logos, then, is a procession from the Father which is founded in an intellectual act. The identity of the Logos is determined solely within the processions and has nothing to do with the otherness of creation, otherness of other beings. The Son's identity is relational and results in the Son's distinction to the Father.

With the person of Jesus who is the Christ in the Gospel of St. John, the prologue introduces the notion of witness. While the Logos does not need a created witness, Jesus of Nazareth does. It is John the Baptist who points him out to the people standing around. In the Prologue the evangelist calls John the witness: "Hic venit in *testimonium*." John was the "martyr" of Jesus of Nazareth, he was the witness, the double. John said that he was not himself the light but that he was a *witness* to the Light. Without this testimony men could not believe in the person of Jesus; they could not believe or know who He is. The dimension of witness is significant here. It is significant throughout John in the many "martyrs" or witnesses to the person of Jesus, either in His signs or in His holiness. Samuel Beckett explores definition of self through the pair: Gogo and Didi, Willie and Winnie, Nagg and Nell, the I and Pim of *How It Is,* the I of *The Unnamable* and Basil, Mahood and Worm. All of these pairs witness the otherness of the person. Consciousness, introspection, the annihilation of the other, are not enough in the determination of self. In the literature studied, the otherness, the "thou" of the witness, is the *sine qua non* for a further attempt at definition. Consciousness and witness, then, are routes in the quest for self-identification that remain simply partial.

The tension between the word or language and the self is a very essential element in *As I Lay Dying* and *Absalom, Absalom!* The storyteller is seeking as much his own identity as the identity of Sutpen in *Absalom, Absalom!,* and all the narratives in a sense are autobiographies of the narrators. While one center of exploration might be Sutpen, another circle could have Quentin in the center trying to emerge through the retelling of the tale. *As I Lay Dying* also states the tension between the language of the self and the deed. Addie constantly wonders about her deception by the word called "love." There are many words which for her mean deception because they do not have an experiential significance. For Anse, love is another word and not a reality. For her friend, Cora, sin as well as salvation are simply vacuous words. For her, it is the reality that is important. She is alive and yet physically dying or dead, while Anse is dead but physically alive.

This tension between word and thought is very significant. St. John says that everything was created through the Word: "Omnia per ipsum facta sunt.'' This signifies a Word which is not empty but that has the creative ability which Eliade and Cassirer refer to when they emphasize the power which comes forth from the naming of an object. The naming calls the presence of the object into being and the word calls for the presence and the creation of its thought. Ordinarily, a person has an idea, a thought, or an insight which he must find the proper words to express. Sometimes, however, he realizes that an insight or an idea is the result of the blocks of words which flow from him. He experiences a feeling of having almost learned something new as he was speaking. The creative force of the word was understood by John. It is this creative force which calls into being something which was not, which gives the meaning, significance, and definition that Quentin seeks. The Unnamable and many of Beckett's ''heroes''—as well as Gide's, Proust's, and Lowry's—are storytellers. They need language to find themselves, to discover themselves. The Unnamable insists that if he stops speaking he will not find himself, while at the same time he is tired of using words. In the silence he does not exist but in the word he does. The Word, or the Logos, in St. John has the power to create. If a person is to find himself in the stories that he tells, in the words that he uses, in his language, he must realize the power of the Logos or the word. Language, then, is another path, although a partial one, to self-definition.

While the person seeks through consciousness, through others, and through his language to find who and where his real self is, he experiences the tension which arises from his many masks. He knows that at times others force him to wear a mask which he decides to accept in response. Yet he realizes that his real self is beyond this multiplicity of masks. The mask is something which transcends history and time and the mutability of life. St. John celebrates the Word incarnated: ''Et Verbum caro factum est.'' The Word takes on flesh. In a sense, the Incarnate Word is the first mask of God. It is John the Baptist who gives witness to the reality behind the mask, however. Pirandello insists on the relativity of the perspective of each person and the mask that each person gives the other. It is only the revelation of self, as Laudisi points out in *Così è (si vi pare)*, that allows one to make the mask pregnable. Yet the mask, madness, and personality are ways of contending with the changing effects that life has on a person. Through the use of the mask in art, a historical personage such as Enrico IV becomes frozen and immutable in his identity. This characterization of the person, as Pirandello points out in his preface, becomes even more real because his identity is more fixed than the author's. The mask is always the visible, although partial, form of the real self. It is that self which has surfaced and become concretized, that Godhead or Self which St. John proclaims finds its mask in the Verbum becoming flesh. The glimpse of God which John speaks of makes its temporal revelation in Jesus of Nazareth who is the Word that transcends time. The relativity of the viewer mistaking feigned madness for madness because of the mask is stressed by Enrico IV of Pirandello. Masks somehow reveal as much to those who know how to see as they obscure or hide. St. John claims that the Word was in the world but the Word was not recognized by some. He was recognized by others who saw beyond the mask to the glory of the Theos. In the analogy which is being used, the mask is a way, a route to the discovery of the glory which is the fuller self.

The reason that the Word is not recognized is that He came into darkness: *"in tenebris."* He is the Light, according to John, Who came into the darkness and was not recognized. Like the search for the self, the path here is labyrinthine. In the myth the creator of the labyrinth, Daedalus, tells Theseus to go back to Ariadne's thread, to go back to himself in order to make his way out of the labyrinth. Theseus follows the advice of Daedalus and returns to himself, discovers that part of self which illumines the dark labyrinth, and establishes the city of wisdom and life, Athens. Gide's telling of the story proclaims that the way out of the labyrinth is the return to the real self, or the finding of the real self which parallels the light in the darkness of the prologue. The only way that the real Logos is discovered is through the realization that it is *His* Light which is the way out of the labyrinth of darkness to life: "In ipso vita erat, et vita erat lux hominum: et lux in tenebris lucet, et tenebrae eam non comprehenderunt" (John 1:4-5). Life means an exit from the darkness; it means Light. Icarus, the son of Daedalus, sought a way out which enticed him into flying too close to the sun. He became the victim of his theologizing and reasoning and ended in death. Since his way out of the labyrinth is *artificial*, he never really manages to escape: instead, so close to the light of the sun, he becomes lost, ironically, in the darkness of the self.

The labyrinth in its symmetries is particularly constructed with contradictions and parallels. Note the beginning and end of *Dans le labyrinthe* in which the narrator contradicts himself about the rain and the sun, the light and the dark. This light and dark imagery is found in the hymn of the prologue, signifying the presence of the Creator in His creation. This is also true of the labyrinth story, as Daedalus, who created the labyrinth, finds himself imprisoned in the labyrinth. Christ, the Word, Who creates the world found Himself in the darkness of the world. He, too, like Daedalus, could only leave by ascension. The creator becomes the victim in the narrative structure of the labyrinth. The hunter becomes the hunted. Borges's short stories like *The Circular Ruins* show that the creator and the created are identified. The emergence from the labyrinth and its path to self are found in the contradictions of light and dark, and in the polarities of self and its maze. In *The Circular Ruins, Borges and I, Tlön, Uqbar, Orbis Tertius,* Borges illustrates this. John in his prologue also allows the Word, the Logos, to escape the darkness of the labyrinth through the proclamation of Him as the Light. Again, while consciousness, language, and the other are avenues of approach toward the definition of self, the search itself is labyrinthine or maze-like, and more than that, the person himself is the maze; he is the word, the maze-like witness of the other and the consciousness of himself. But what is even more significant, he is the Creator.

The person ultimately is one who is creating himself as he lives. Unlike his masks he has no fixed form. His language constantly forces him on. His consciousness constantly brings him new data about himself. Out of the maze of possibilities, he becomes who he is. The impossibility of ever reaching adequate definition is based on the fact that the person is "not yet"; that is, he is becoming. He seeks to understand himself through his many poses, through introspection, through the judgments of others about him, through his functions. And he realizes that all of this is inadequate and only partial. Thus, he creates himself. In the prologue, the Word, the Logos, is the *"agens mediator."* The Word is not only the mediator of Creation; however, He is also the Revealer or the Narrator: "Deum nemo vidit unquam: unigenitus Filius, qui est in sinu Patris, ipse enarravit" (John 1 :18). No one can see the Father except the Son who reveals the Father, who tells of Him. In *Les Faux-Monnayeurs* of André Gide, artistic creation is the key to the wedding of the form and the content of the novel. While Edouard, the novelist, is creating his own *Les Faux-Monnayeurs,* he wonders who he is; André Gide, his creator, claims that he too is becoming: "I never am, I become. I become what I believe (or what you believe) I am."[5] This becoming is essentially the creative energy which lies within the person and constitutes the difficulty of any attempt at complete definition. In every literary creation the author has at least one created second self who is his mask and who ironically becomes his creator by being the organizing force of his activity. It is through the creations or the masks that the author is revealed. Pirandello states this in his preface to *Sei personaggi,* as does Gide in his journals and Edouard in his journals. They show how their masks, their personae, their fictive selves, are revelations. It is the Word who reveals the self in John's prologue. He is both the *"agens mediator"* and the revealer of the Theos, or the first self.[6]

In conclusion, the creator is that self who is constantly becoming. He ever eludes definition and imprisonment. He may be the victim of the dark labyrinth, but he cannot be contained within his creation. He transcends it through his freely chosen masks as well as through the projected masks of others. He knows himself through his consciousness and through his relationships with the other. He is defined less in terms of opposition, less in terms of "I am not he," and more in terms of how much he is the other. Through his consciousness of self he first learns that he must make a quest and then continues to find in the wasteland a double who is his witness. He realizes that he is more than his functions and his masks, although they may be attractive distractions. He knows he must make his way out of the labyrinth and not enclose himself within his own questionings; he must seek to become himself. He is constantly in search, he is the one who continues to be open to all the possibilities which self offers. The persona or the myth of the self is a fiction of the creator which allows the creator to say "I" to his many "children." He is the first storyteller, who is writing his own history in relationships which extend ever outward. He is one who through his many fictive lives becomes who he is. At the least he is one who realizes that he is not yet. As Laudisi wonders while looking into his glass, seeing his projection, "Who is the real Laudisi?," as Borges asks in *Borges and I,* "Who is the real author?" so, too, the reader wonders in reading Edouard's journals in *Les Faux-Monnayeurs* as well as in reading Gide's version, "Where is the real author?" The real author is there, but his presence escapes both himself and his viewer so that he can always remain one who is on his way. He is one who is continually in search. As Siddhartha continues searching for his self in many different areas, so every person continues. It is only after the person has searched and realized the "not yet" quality, the becoming, the possibilities of his person, that he can be at peace. Siddhartha begins his journey in this way, with the same kinds of questions; he asks himself whether his own reality must be found within himself.[7] He, too, seeks his existence within, as do Murphy and Monsieur Teste. He also learns, however, that it is not only found within but must be sought outside. It must be sought through his relations with the other which he learned through Kamala. While he learned through much suffering and search, his friend Govinda learned from him. Kissing Siddhartha, Govinda sees and understands where the self that both of them sought is. He sees it in the face of his friend who becomes fused with a multitude: "He no longer saw his friend Siddhartha's face, but instead he saw other faces, many of them, a long series, flowing like a stream of faces, hundreds, thousands that came and went, and yet seemed to be there all together, constantly changing and renewing themselves, yet all unmistakably the one Siddhartha" (p. 120). Govinda also sees animals, children, a murderer; he sees all kinds of faces and forms and relationships in this one moment. And in this one moment that he sees Siddhartha, he sees everyone. He sees himself and yet no one. He glimpsed in the face of Siddhartha all the faces that made up his life and that make up everyone's lives: "And yet none of them died, they only changed and were constantly reborn, constantly wore new faces, but with no passage of time between one face and the next" (p. 120). It is as if these faces all become one; they are all participants in the one face which is distinct and yet contains infinity:

> And all these forms and faces rested, flowed, gave birth to new ones, swam past and merged with one another, and over them all remained something thin, unreal, and yet existing, extended like thin ice or glass, like a transparent skin, shell, form, or mask: it was Siddhartha's smiling face, which he, Govinda in this precise moment touched with his lips. (P. 120).

It is eventually through the mask of Siddhartha's face that Govinda sees all men, becomes all men and becomes himself. The mask and the fictions of self allow Govinda and his real self to penetrate the mystery of all the selves of the universe: how everyone is related to everyone, how the consciousness of the individual pierces through to the core of reality, how the witness of the faces of the other tells the story of the existence of the self, how the labyrinth ceases to be a mystery because the Creator has escaped it. The creator is the self who is everything and nothing at the same time. The person and the self defined as a process, defined as relational, participate in the great cosmic mystery, becoming many and no one. He is, as God tells Shakespeare in "Everything and Nothing" by Borges, everyone and no one:

History adds that before or after dying he found himself in the presence of God and told Him: "I who have been so many men in vain want to be one and myself." The voice of the Lord answered from a whirlwind: "Neither am I anyone; I have dreamt the world as you dreamt your work, my Shakespeare, and among the forms in my dream are you, who like myself are many and no one."[8]

This self is the ultimate revelation which the Word makes, which the first mask of God narrates. It is this self which is in constant need of rediscovery and creation by the person. Some rightly see this self in modern literature as vestigial.[9] While the self is in eclipse, the revelation continues. The person continues to assert his presence as an end. The self has his witnesses, his consciousness, his masks. It is they who have seen him and who reveal his sometimes hidden and eclipsed presence, his Transcendence and his Immanence (John 1:18). The mystery of the self, then, is one of a continual revelation which transcends time in the words "not yet," and which can never be contained because the self is related to an infinity of faces not yet dreamt or created.

NOTES

INDEX

# NOTES

## INTRODUCTION

1. Hanna Charney, "Le Héros anonyme: De Monsieur Teste aux Mandarins," *Romanic Review*, 1 (December 1959), p. 268.
2. Miguel de Unamuno, "The Man of Flesh and Bone," *Tragic Sense of Life*, trans. J. E. Crawford Flitch (New York, Dover, 1954), p. 9.
3. *Ibid.*, pp. 8–9.
4. Theodore L. Gross, *Representative Man* (New York, Free Press, 1970), p. 4. For a discussion of the Aristotelian hero cf. Northrop Frye, *Anatomy of Criticism* (New York, Atheneum, 1967), pp. 33–67.
5. Maurice Merleau-Ponty, "Man, the Hero," *Sense and Non-Sense* (Northwestern University Press, 1964), p. 182.
6. Herman Melville, *Moby Dick* (New York, Airmont, 1964), p. 55.
7. Albert Camus, *La Peste* (Paris, Gallimard, 1962), p. 1403.
8. James Joyce, *A Portrait of the Artist as a Young Man* (New York, Viking, 1964), p. 117.
9. Ian Watt, "Realism and the Novel Form," in *Approaches to the Novel*, ed. Robert Scholes (San Francisco: Chandler Publishing Co., 1966), p. 83. Cf. Harry Levin, "Realism in Perspective," in *Approaches to the Novel*. Cf. Erich Auerbach's *Mimesis*, trans. Willard R. Trask (Princeton, Princeton University Press, 1968).
10. Dimitri Chizhevsky, "The Theme of the Double in Dostoevsky," in *Dostoevsky*, ed. René Wellek (Englewood Cliffs, Prentice Hall, 1962), pp. 112–130.
11. Hermann Hesse, *Siddhartha* (Frankfurt, Rowohlt, 1950), p. 9.
12. Miguel Serrano, *C. G. Jung and Hermann Hesse* (New York, Schocken, 1966), pp. 82–83.

## CHAPTER 1

1. Erik H. Erikson, *Identity* (New York, Norton, 1968), p. 217.
2. R. D. Laing, *The Divided Self* (Baltimore, Penguin, 1965), p. 158.

3. Erikson, *Identity*, p. 19.

4. A study of the identity problem of youth in modern literature deserves separate treatment. Proust, Alain Fournier, Radiguet, Martin du Gard, Mauriac, and Joyce are among the modern writers who explore the problem of maturing to a sense of selfhood in the adolescent.

5. Louise Vinge, *The Narcissus Theme in Western European Literature up to the Early 19th Century,* trans. from the Swedish by Robert Dewsnap in collaboration with Lisbeth Grönlund and by Nigel Reeves in collaboration with Ingrid Söderberg-Reeves (Lund, Gleerups, 1967), p. 313.

6. Ovid, *The Metamorphoses,* vol. I, bk. III, trans. Dryden, Pope, Congreve, Addison, and Others (London, Valpy, 1833), p. 86.

7. Jean Paul Sartre, *Nausea,* trans. Lloyd Alexander (New York, New Directions, 1964), p. 29.

8. Agnes Ethel Mackey, *The Universal Self* (London, Routledge and Kegan Paul, 1961).

9. Paul Valéry, *Note et digression, Oeuvres,* I (Paris: Bibliothèque de la Pléiade, 1957), 1223.

10. Paul Valéry, *Introduction à la méthode de Léonard de Vinci, Oeuvres,* I, 1155.

11. Paul Valéry, *Léonard et les philosophes, Oeuvres,* I, 1225.

12. *Ibid.,* pp. 1226–27.

13. Paul Valéry, *Monsieur Teste, Oeuvres,* II, 64.

14. *Ibid.,* pp. 66–67.

15. *Ibid.,* p. 14.

16. *Ibid.,* p. 66.

17. Valéry, *Note et digression, Oeuvres,* I, 1228.

18. *Ibid.,* p. 1226.

19. *Ibid.,* p. 1229.

20. *Ibid.,* p. 1228.

21. *Ibid.,* p. 1229.

22. Valéry, *Monsieur Teste, Oeuvres,* II, 44.

23. Paul Valéry, *La Jeune Parque, Oeuvres,* I, 97.

24. Valéry, *Monsieur Teste, Oeuvres,* II, 64.

25. *Ibid.,* p. 74.

26. *Ibid.,* pp. 74–75.

27. *Ibid.,* p. 28.

28. Valéry, *Note et digression, Oeuvres,* I, 1230. Although some readers like to identify Leonardo or Monsieur Teste with one another and with the author, Paul Valéry reminds the reader in a note that the life of the author is not the life of the character. This applies not only to the relationship of Monsieur Teste to Valéry but also that of Murphy to Samuel Beckett whom some critics have sought to equate. The author and his characters diverge. Furthermore, Monsieur Teste as well as his author are distinct from the man, Valéry: "I was forced to invent a character capable of producing many works. My obsession was that, where people and things were concerned, I was interested exclusively in their function; and when it came to works of art, my interest ran exclusively toward the act of their creation. I knew that such works as I would create would inevitably be falsifications and hybrid constructions, since their *author,* fortunately, is never the *man.*"

29. Samuel Beckett, *Murphy* (New York, Grove Press, 1957), p. 4.

30. Samuel Beckett, *Watt* (New York, Grove Press, 1959), p. 166.

31. *Ibid.*
32. Cf. Jacqueline Hoefer, *"Watt," Perspective,* 2 (Autumn 1959), 166–182.
33. Samuel Beckett, *Three Novels* (New York, Grove Press, 1965), p. 15.
34. Beckett, *Three Novels,* p. 42.
35. *Ibid.,* p. 170.
36. Samuel I. Mintz, "Beckett's Murphy: A 'Cartesian' Novel," *Perspective,* 2 (Autumn 1959), p. 165.
37. Mintz, "Beckett's Murphy," p. 165.
38. René Descartes extended to man, himself, the dualism which has haunted man from the time when he was first able to distinguish light from darkness. He explained that body and mind are two separate substances: mind is a thinking substance, body a corporeal substance. Between body and mind there is interaction but not real unity. It is the mind which tells the body that it exists and in some sort of union proclaims *"cogito, ergo sum."* His methodology was framed to bring about true and exact propositions from this fundamental principle. See René Descartes, *The Philosophical Works of Descartes,* tr. E. S. Haldane and G. R. T. Ross (New York, Dover, 1955), I, p. 101: "But immediately afterwards, I noticed that whilst I thus wished to think all things false, it was absolutely essential that the I who thought this should be somewhat, and remarking that this truth 'I think, therefore I am' was so certain and so assured that all the most extravagant suppositions brought forward by the sceptics were incapable of shaking it." The methodology of Descartes was developed from the principle of the cogito as an apologia for reason. The dualism which he suggested in his system was further developed by Arnold Geulincx. The mind for Geulincx did not dialogue with or control the body; it could exercise control only over itself. Consequently, the needs of the body should be disdained and man must logically retreat to his mind. "Ubi nihil vales, etiam ibi nihil veles" becomes the motto for this type of existence. Murphy, a disciple of Geulincx, practiced this philosophy. His guiding principle was "ubi nihil vales, ibi etiam nihil velis" (Arnold Geulincx, *Metaphysica Vera Pars Prima, Opera Philosophica,* II (The Hague, Martinus Nijhoff, 1892), p. 155. The whole quotation is as follows (the translation is mine): "My human condition is entirely independent of me. This exposition reveals itself in ethics and is the mouth of the river of morality. It follows from these words: Since we are worth nothing in human fortune, we wish for nothing. Here, therefore, is the first, highest and most general principle that makes up morality, the foundation of ethics, known clearly through the light of nature: where you are powerless to do anything, here also you do not wish for anything." Other dualistic philosophers carried the split in man further. Malebranche, for instance, claimed that the body is a machine chained to the soul. His doctrine leads to a concept of causality which is merely occasional. This very brief and sketchy summary of dualistic philosophical teaching shows how, in the doctrine of Geulincx and in some of the dualists, life could be carried on and should be carried on in the mind itself since the body cannot be managed and the outside world can be controlled still less.
39. Beckett, *Murphy,* p. 2, followed by French translation from Samuel Beckett, *Murphy* (Paris, Les Editions de Minuit, 1967), p. 8.

## CHAPTER 2

1. Martin Buber, *I and Thou,* trans. Ronald Gregor Smith (New York, Scribner's, 1958).

2. *Ibid.,* p. 62.

3. Gabriel Marcel, "The Drama of the Soul in Exile," in *Three Plays,* trans. Rosalind Heywood (New York, Hill and Wang, 1965), p. 16.

4. *Ibid.,* pp. 31–32.

5. Samuel Beckett, *Poems in English* (New York, Grove Press, 1964), pp. 49–50.

6. Samuel Beckett, *Waiting for Godot* (New York, Grove Press, 1954), p. 94.

7. *Ibid.,* p. 82.

8. *Ibid.,* p. 64.

9. *Ibid.,* p. 68.

10. Samuel Beckett, *Endgame* (New York, Grove Press, 1958), p. 81.

11. *Ibid.,* p. 83.

12. *Ibid.,* p. 62.

13. *Ibid.,* p. 78.

14. *Ibid.,* p. 79.

15. Samuel Beckett, *Happy Days* (New York, Grove Press, 1961), p. 64.

16. Samuel Beckett, *How It Is* (New York, Grove Press, 1961), p. 7.

17. *Ibid.,* p. 56.

18. Richard Coe, *Samuel Beckett* (New York, Grove Press, 1964), p. 84.

19. Beckett, *How It Is,* pp. 55–56.

20. *Ibid.,* p. 112.

21. *Ibid.,* pp. 118–119.

22. *Ibid.,* pp. 145–146.

23. Beckett, *Endgame,* p. 69.

24. Samuel Beckett, *Three Novels* (New York, Grove Press, 1955), p. 414.

25. Beckett, *Endgame,* p. 69.

26. Beckett, *Three Novels,* p. 414.

27. Beckett, *Endgame,* p. 69.

28. Beckett, *Three Novels,* p. 414.

29. Beckett, *Endgame,* p. 69.

30. *Ibid.,* p. 81.

31. The literature of Samuel Beckett up to this point, while scatological at times, is not at all fulfillingly erotic, and the couple or the pair are not related to one another sexually. Their attempts at love or sex are very feeble expressions of contact. There is, however, a whole gamut of attempts at self-definition through fulfilling sexual expression. Particular examples could be cited from the literature of D. H. Lawrence, Alberto Moravia, and even Lawrence Durrell. The double or the other in a sexual relation suggests the link toward a self which is searching for its own definition. For a person to really be complete, his relationship to the other must also mean an organic wholeness. Signifying life, the sexual aspects which go into the completing of the person are beautifully portrayed in the words of D. H. Lawrence. Involved in this process of communication is the emergence into conscious being and into a fuller life to which the sexual relationship leads. For instance, in *The Man Who Died* the wedding of Christian and Western myths, between Jesus and Osiris, Jesus and Isis also signifies a wedding of selves which makes for wholeness. D. H. Lawrence expresses it in this way: "And Church doctrine teaches the resurrection of the

body; and if that doesn't mean the whole man, what does it mean? And if man is whole without a woman . . . then I'm damned" (D. H. Lawrence, *The Letters of D. H. Lawrence,* ed. Aldous Huxley [New York, Viking, 1932], pp. 786–787). Admirably expressed by Mark Spilka in *The Love Ethic of D. H. Lawrence,* this progression of the individual in his relationship to the other is one which involves wholeness, life and the identity of the individual in his relationship to the other. D. H. Lawrence describes this integrity of the person this way: "You can develop an instinct for life . . . an instinct of the whole consciousness in a man, bodily, mental, spiritual at once. And only in the novel are *all* things given full play . . . For out of the full play of all things emerges the only thing that is anything, the wholeness of a man, the wholeness of a woman, man alive, and live woman." (D. H. Lawrence, *Phoenix: The Posthumous Papers of D. H. Lawrence* [New York, Viking, 1936], p. 538.)

Between the world of D. H. Lawrence and that of Samuel Beckett there is a vast chasm. However, still present in Samuel Beckett is the need for completion, for identity, for a witness to life itself that the other provides. Samuel Beckett's literature may almost seem posterotic. His heroes are so disintegrated that their search for fulfillment and identity is ludicrous. Fragments of selves, they are simply the shadows of the characters of the realistic novel in which sexual expression is possible. While the doubles, the couples, and the pairs of Beckett try to relate to one another, they experience mere illusions of the kind of sexual expression which allows for wholeness. Gogo and Didi trying to embrace, Willie and Winnie, seeking to make love, are very distant echoes of the organic wholeness which comes from a personal encounter. The significance here is that the echo and shadow are present so long as man still needs to say "I" to an existence which is his.

CHAPTER 3

1. Claude Lévi-Strauss, *Structural Anthropology* (Garden City, Doubleday, 1967), pp. 200–208. *Langue* belongs to a reversible time and *parole* to a non-reversible time (p. 205).

2. *Ibid.,* p. 206.

3. *Ibid.*

4. *Ibid.,* p. 207.

5. *Ibid.,* p. 227.

6. Bronislaw Malinowski, *Magic, Science and Religion* (Garden City, Doubleday, 1954), p. 101. "Studied alive, myth is not symbolic, but a direct expression of its subject matter; it is not an explanation in satisfaction of a scientific interest, but a narrative resurrection of the primeval reality, told in satisfaction of deep religious wants, moral cravings, social submissions, assertions, even practical requirements. Myth fulfills in primitive culture an indispensable function; it safeguards and enforces morality; it expresses, enhances, and codifies belief; it vouches for the guidance of man. Myth is thus a vital ingredient of human civilization; it is not an idle tale, but a hard-worked active force; it is not an intellectual explanation or an artistic imagery, but a pragmatic charter of primitive faith and moral wisdom."

7. Mircea Eliade, *Myth and Reality* (New York, Harper and Row, 1963), p. 108.

8. *Ibid.,* p. 5.

9. *Ibid.*, p. 141.

10. *Ibid.*

11. Ernst Cassirer, *An Essay on Man* (New Haven, Yale University Press, 1944), p. 109.

12. Ernst Cassirer, *Language and Myth* (New York, Dover, 1946), p. viii.

13. *Ibid.*, p. 8.

14. *Ibid.*, pp. 49–50.

15. *Ibid.*, p. 58.

16. *Ibid.*, p. 61.

17. *Ibid.*, p. 81.

18. Bernard J. F. Lonergan, S.J., *Insight: A Study of Human Understanding* (London, Longmans, Green, 1957), p. 547.

19. *Ibid.*, pp. 542–543.

20. *Ibid.*, p. 548.

21. *Ibid.*, p. 545.

22. Northrop Frye, *Fables of Identity* (New York, Harcourt, Brace and World, 1963), "Myth, Fiction and Displacement," p. 21.

23. *Ibid.*, p. 22.

24. *Ibid.*, p. 32.

25. *Ibid.*, p. 33.

26. *Ibid.*, p. 36.

27. *Ibid.*, p. 38.

28. Northrop Frye, *Anatomy of Criticism* (New York, Atheneum, 1967), "Theory of Myths," p. 136.

29. *Ibid.*, p. 136.

30. Northrop Frye, *A Study of English Romanticism* (New York, Random House, 1968), p. 8.

31. *Ibid.*, p. 12.

32. *Ibid.*, p. 46.

33. Susan Sontag, *Against Interpretation* (New York, Dell, 1961), p. 18.

34. *Ibid.*, p. 19.

35. Frederick J. Hoffman, *Samuel Beckett: The Language of Self* (New York, Dutton, 1964), p. 80.

36. Samuel Beckett, *The Unnamable* (New York, Grove Press, 1965), p. 303.

37. *The Jerusalem Bible* (New York, Doubleday, 1966), 2 Samuel 19:5.

38. William Faulkner, *Absalom, Absalom!* (New York, Random House, 1951), p. 10.

39. William Faulkner, *Faulkner in the University* (New York, Vintage Books, 1959), pp. 273–274.

40. Faulkner, *Absalom, Absalom!*, pp. 8–9.

41. *Jerusalem Bible*, 2 Samuel 13:24.

42. Olga Vickery, *The Novels of William Faulkner* (Baton Rouge, Louisiana State University Press, 1964), p. 52.

43. William Faulkner, *As I Lay Dying* (New York, Modern Library, 1946), p. 460.

44. Vickery, *The Novels of William Faulkner*, p. 53.

45. Faulkner, *As I Lay Dying*, pp. 465–466.

46. James Joyce, *Finnegans Wake* (New York, Viking, 1965), pp. 628 and 3.

47. Marcel Proust, *Du côté de chez Swann* (Paris, Editions Gallimard, 1954), p. 8.

48. *Ibid.*, p. 7.

49. Mircea Eliade, *Myth and Reality* (New York, Harper & Row, 1968), p. 6.
50. *Ibid.*

## CHAPTER 4

1. Luigi Pirandello, *Così è (se vi pare)*, *Maschere nude*, II (Milan, Arnoldo Mondadori, 1952), 260–261.
2. *Ibid.*, p. 220.
3. *Ibid.*, p. 197.
4. *Ibid.*, pp. 224–225.
5. Pirandello, *Enrico IV, Maschere nude*, II, 539.
6. *Ibid.*, p. 540.
7. *Ibid.*, pp. 542–543.
8. *Ibid.*, p. 545.
9. *Ibid.*, p. 555.
10. Pirandello, *Prefazione: Sei personaggi in cerca d'autore, Maschere nude*, I, 14.
11. Pirandello, *Sei personaggi*, p. 55.
12. Umberto Cantoro, *Luigi Pirandello e il problema della personalità* (Bologna, Gallo, 1954), p. 23.
13. *Ibid.*, p. 25.
14. *Ibid.*, p. 23.
15. Lawrence Durrell, *Balthazar* (New York, Dutton, 1961), pp. 14–15.
16. William Faulkner, *Absalom, Absalom!* (New York, Modern Library, 1951), p. 261.

## CHAPTER 5

1. P. Ovidius Nason, *Metamorphoseon Liber VIII*, "Ariadne in Coronam," *Fabula II, P. Ovidii Nasonis Opera Omnia* (London, Valpy, 1821), pp. 1292–1293.
2. *Ibid., Fabula III,* "Perdix in Avem sui nominis," p. 1295.
3. *Ibid.*, pp. 1297–1298.
4. Edith Hamilton, *Mythology* (New York, Mentor, 1962), pp. 149–158.
5. Paul G. Kuntz, "What Daedalus Told Ariadne, or, How to Escape the Labyrinth," *Monist*, 50 (October 1966), 504.
6. *Ibid.*
7. Albert Guerard sees Gide's *Thésée* as a restatement of Gide's humanistic individualism. Many years in the planning and a type of spiritual autobiography, *Thésée* results from Gide's confidence that, after a lifetime of conflict with it, his philosophy would survive. "Any reader can work out, to his amusement, the witty parallels between Theseus' adventure and Gide's own. Theseus too went through a period of relaxed hedonism; then recognized, in sharp reaction, the value of discipline and effort. As a youth he too was timid in society. But he was sufficiently assured to see that he owed something to himself, as well as to Ariadne. His sexual preferences run counter to the accepted ethics of the time; convention demanded a homosexual affair with Glaucos. But he takes Phaedra instead, disguised in Glaucos' clothes. He is strengthened by his belief

in progress but also by discipline; he realizes that after the time for adventure and self-discovery must come the time for rule" (Albert J. Guerard, *André Gide* [Cambridge, Mass., Harvard University Press, 1951], p. 91).

8. André Gide, *Thésée, Romans, Récits et Soties, Oeuvres Lyriques* (Paris, Gallimard, 1958), p. 1432.

9. Miguel Serrano, *C. G. Jung and Hermann Hesse* (New York, Schocken, 1966), pp. 82–83.

10. *Ibid.*, p. 83.

11. *Ibid.*, p. 84.

12. *Ibid.*, p. 101.

13. Gide, *Thésée*, p. 1438.

14. *Ibid.*, p. 1448.

15. Ana Maria Barrenechea, *Borges the Labyrinth Maker* (New York, New York University Press, 1965), p. 60.

16. Jorge Luis Borges, "Valéry as Symbol," in *Labyrinths* (New York, New Directions, 1964), p. 197.

17. Jorge Luis Borges, "The Library of Babel," in *Labyrinths*, p. 54.

18. *Ibid.*

19. Jorge Luis Borges, "The Immortal," in *Labyrinths*, p. 107.

20. *Ibid.*, p. 109.

21. Jorge Luis Borges, "The Circular Ruins," in *Labyrinths*, p. 50.

22. Borges, "The Immortal," p. 110.

23. Jorge Luis Borges, "The Garden of Forking Paths," in *Labyrinths*, p. 28.

24. Jorge Luis Borges, *El Hacedor* (Buenos Aires, Emecé, 1960), p. 111.

25. Jorge Luis Borges, "Borges and I," in *Labyrinths*, pp. 246–247.

26. Jorge Luis Borges, "Everything and Nothing," in *Labyrinths*, p. 43.

27. Jorge Luis Borges, "The God's Script," in *Labyrinths*, p. 172.

28. Alain Robbe-Grillet, *Pour un nouveau roman* (Paris, Les Editions de Minuit, 1963), p. 147.

29. *Ibid.*, p. 152.

30. *Ibid.*, p. 119.

31. *Ibid.*, p. 149.

32. *Ibid.*, p. 142.

33. Alain Robbe-Grillet, *Dans le labyrinthe* (Paris, Les Editions de Minuit, 1959), p. 9.

34. Alain Robbe-Grillet, *Le Voyeur* (Paris, Les Editions de Minuit, 1955), p. 9.

35. Bruce Morrissette, *Les Romans de Robbe-Grillet* (Paris, Les Editions de Minuit, 1963), p. 87.

36. Robbe-Grillet, *Le Voyeur*, pp. 15–16.

37. R. M. Albérès, *Métamorphoses du roman* (Paris, Editions Albin Michel, 1966), p. 258.

38. *Ibid.*, p. 266.

39. Robbe-Grillet, *Le Voyeur*, p. 222.

40. Gide, *Thésée*, p. 1453.

41. Robbe-Grillet, *Dans le labyrinthe*, p. 221.

42. Gide, *Thésée*, p. 1453.

## CHAPTER 6

1. Carlos Lynes, "André Gide and the Problem of Form in the Novel," in *Forms of Modern Fiction,* ed. William Van O'Connor (Bloomington, Indiana: Indiana University Press, 1964), p. 188.
2. Georges Brachfield, "The Novel of Ideas," in *Approaches to the Twentieth-Century Novel,* ed. John Unterecker (New York, Crowell, 1965), p. 153.
3. *Ibid.,* p. 188.
4. André Gide, *Journal* (Paris, Gallimard, 1954), I, 832.
5. *Ibid.,* p. 794.
6. André Gide, *Journal des Faux-Monnayeurs* (Paris, Gallimard, 1927), p. 96.
7. Gide, *Journal,* I, 879.
8. André Gide, *Les Faux-Monnayeurs, Romans* (Paris, Gallimard, 1958), p. 1096.
9. *Ibid.,* p. 1142.
10. *Ibid.,* p. 1081.
11. *Ibid.,* p. 1086.
12. *Ibid.,* p. 987.
13. *Ibid.,* p. 1007.
14. Gide, *Journal,* I, 852.
15. *Ibid.*
16. Gide, *Les Faux-Monnayeurs,* pp. 1093–1094.
17. *Ibid.,* p. 1108.
18. *Ibid.,* 1109.
19. Gide, *Journal,* I, 801.
20. Wayne C. Booth, *The Rhetoric of Fiction* (Chicago, University of Chicago Press, 1961), pp. 70–71.
21. *Ibid.,* p. 73.
22. It is interesting to note that Albert J. Guerard finds that the opening chapters of *Les Faux-Monnayeurs* and parts of *Les Caves du Vatican* are among the triumphs of modern antirealism. *L'Immoraliste,* on the other hand, he calls one of the greatest realistic novels of the century (Albert J. Guerard, *André Gide* [Cambridge, Mass., Harvard University Press, 1951], p. 175).
23. "In one sense, it can be said that in any poem there is not one persona but several. Co-existent and almost inextricably entangled with one another are several points of view each of which qualifies and complicates the autonomy of the others, and none of which is ever quite identical with the poet" (George T. Wright, *The Poet in the Poem* [Berkeley and Los Angeles, University of California Press, 1962], p. 23).
24. Guerard, *André Gide,* p. 162.

## CHAPTER 7

1. Alain Robbe-Grillet, *Pour un nouveau roman* (Paris, Les Editions de Minuit, 1963), "Nouveau Roman, homme nouveau," p. 146.
2. Eugene Goodheart, *The Cult of the Ego* (Chicago, University of Chicago Press, 1968), p. 198.
3. Robbe-Grillet, p. 147.
4. *Ibid.*

5. *Ibid.*, p. 149.

6. André Gide, *Les Faux-Monnayeurs, Romans* (Paris, Gallimard, 1958), p. 1108.

7. William Faulkner, *The Sound and the Fury* (New York, Modern Library, 1929), p. 23.

8. *Ibid.*, p. 95.

9. *Ibid.*, p. 198.

10. *Ibid.*, p. 281.

11. Marcel Proust, *Cities of the Plain* in *Remembrance of Things Past,* trans. C. K. Scott Moncrieff (New York, Random House, 1932), II, 114.

12. The narrator points out in the following magnificent passage at the end of the novel how an understanding of Time relates to the form of the novel about the self: "And in truth, all these different planes on which Time, since I had come to grasp its meaning again at this reception, was arranging the different periods of my life, thereby bringing me to realise that in a book which aimed to recount a human life one would have to use, in contrast to the 'plane' psychology ordinarily employed, a sort of three-dimensional, 'solid' psychology, added a fresh beauty to the resurrections of the past which my memory had evoked as I sat musing alone in the library, because memory, by bringing the past into the present unmodified, just as it appeared when it was itself the present, eliminates precisely that great dimension of Time which governs the fullest realisation of our lives" (Marcel Proust, *The Past Recaptured,* trans. Frederick A. Blossom in *Remembrance of Things Past,* trans. C. K. Moncrieff, II, 1111.)

13. Jean-Paul Sartre, *Literature and Existentialism,* trans. Bernard Frechtman (New York, Citadel, 1949), p. 61.

14. *Ibid.*, p. 45.

15. Edwin Honig, *Dark Conceit* (New York, Oxford University Press, 1966), p. 67.

16. Malcolm Lowry, *Under the Volcano* (New York, New American Library, 1966), pp. 391–392.

17. Vladimir Nabokov, *Pale Fire* (New York, Berkley Medallion Books, 1968), p. 18.

18. *Ibid.*, p. 212.

19. Alain Robbe-Grillet, *La Jalousie* (Paris, Les Editions de Minuit, 1957), p. 79.

20. Samuel Beckett, *Murphy* (New York, Grove Press, 1957), p. 1.

21. Samuel Beckett, *Three Novels* (New York, Grove Press, 1957), p. 29.

22. Samuel Beckett, *How It Is* (New York, Grove Press, 1964), p. 7.

23. Robbe-Grillet, "Samuel Beckett ou la présence sur la scène," *Pour un nouveau roman,* p. 121.

24. *Ibid.*, p. 122.

25. Samuel Beckett, *Endgame* (New York, Grove Press, 1959), p. 71.

26. Miguel Serrano, *C. G. Jung & Hermann Hesse* (New York, Schocken, 1966), p. 22.

27. Robbe-Grillet, *Pour un nouveau roman,* p. 152.

## CONCLUSION

1. The emphasis on the not-yet quality of man's self-definition brings to the mind of the reader of contemporary philosophy the name of Ernst Bloch. Bloch applies the brief logical statement "S is not yet P" to man who is con-

stantly becoming, never totally fulfilled, always transcending himself.

Never completely within grasp, man's essence must always remain in a "not-yet" condition. A mystery to himself, each person is still unfinished and is never completely known even to himself, obscurely reliving the history of mankind in himself. Bloch states that we do not own our true existence; we do not know who sleeps in the dark room we call I. In quoting Ulysses's cry to Polyphemus, "My name is Nobody," Bloch believes that for purposes of final identification this must always remain the human name (Ernst Bloch, *Man on His Own,* trans. E. B. Ashton [New York, Herder and Herder, 1970], "Karl Marx, Death and the Apocalypse," p. 52).

In the essay entitled *"Incipit Vita Nova"* Bloch stresses that man's task must be to illumine the predication of the obscure *existere* in everything, which is a predication made to the what of a still undiscovered essence. Implicit in the philosophy of the "not-yet" of Bloch is the necessity to search for the self in obscurity, ever hopeful of the possibilities which the future can bring. This "not-yet" condition of the person is linked to the "not-yet" condition of society, looking to politics as well as art to discover and create new identities of peoples as well as of the person. The maxim *Principius obsta* here is the corollary to *Incipit vita nuova;* for man must keep faith with the beginning, whose genesis is yet to arrive. In this context, he claims, Prometheus becomes the foremost model not simply as a thief or rebel but as a hopeful adventurer: "The most inalienable of all categories for the development of our life, literature, philosophy and practice are certainly man holding himself upright and the as yet undetermined and undeveloped actual content of his potentiality" (Ernst Bloch, *"Incipit Vita Nuova,"* p. 91). With the courage of an adventurer the I can creatively make the exitus-exodus in the collective we. Here the I becomes objective "by joining itself like a violin string to thousands of things and social facts it encounters, on the basis of their vacillation and vacuity—an objectivation that will, of course, make the 'I' in itself ring more fully, widely, and deeply" (Ernst Bloch, "Karl Marx, Death and the Apocalypse," p. 47).

2. Donatius Mollat, *Introductio in Exegesim Scriptorum Sancti Joannis* (Rome, Pontificia Universitas Gregoriana, 1962).

3. Bernard Lonergan, *Divinarum Personarum* (Rome, Pontificia Universitas Gregoriana, 1959), p. 59.

4. *Ibid.,* p. 61.

5. André Gide, *Journal* (Paris, Gallimard, 1954), I, 852.

6. During the act of creation, the creator may experience himself as another person to such an extent that he may use other names to define his work, particularly if the creations, too, seem so different from each other. One way of escaping the *finiteness* of being tied to a center with one name and, therefore, permitting self-transcendence is to invent heteronyms which even if added together cannot explain the mystery of the creative self. Fernando Pessoa is a modern poet who does precisely this and invents the heteronyms for poems which reveal the distinct lives of the different poets within him. For Caeiro, Reiss, and de Campos he creates independent lives, capable from their experience of explaining the poetry which comes from not any one of them, and yet from a center which encompasses all of them at once. Unconsciously, Pessoa does what theologians describe in their explanations of the diverse action of the Trinity; they attribute to one Person the work which characterize the unique qualities which come from his relationship in the Godhead. For instance, works of charity, love, and grace are ascribed to the Holy Spirit since his relation-

ship in the Trinity originates in Love, while creation seems to be the work of the Father and the ultimate judgment the work of the Son. Yet, at times, each does the work of the other, overlapping into a center that goes beyond all of them and resides in the mystery of Infinity.

7. Hermann Hesse, *Siddhartha* (Frankfurt, Rowohlt, 1950), p. 9.

8. Jorge Luis Borges, "Everything and Nothing," in *Labyrinths* (New York, New Directions, 1962), p. 249.

9. Wylie Sypher, *Loss of the Self* (New York, Random House, 1962).

# INDEX

167

# Index

DATE DUE

DEMCO, INC. 38-3012